Douglas John Hall

When You *Pray*

Thinking
Your Way
into
God's World

Judson Press ® Valley Forge

Unless otherwise indicated, Bible quotations in this volume are from the Revised Standard Version of the Bible, copyrighted 1946, 1952(c), 1971, 1973 by the Division of Christian Education of the National Council of the Churches of Christ in the U.S.A., and used by permission.

Library of Congress Cataloging-in-Publication Data

Hall, Douglas John, 1928-
    When you pray.

    Includes bibliographical references.
    1. Prayer. I. Title.
BV210.2.H34 1987   248.3'2   87-2695
ISBN 0-8170-1105-6 (pbk.)

The name JUDSON PRESS is registered as a trademark in the U.S. Patent Office.
Printed in the U.S.A.

To Doris J. Dyke

for her "Intimations of Maturity"

" . . . our Christian existence will be confined today to only two things: prayer and acting justly among men. All thinking, speaking, and organizing of the things of Christianity must be born out of this praying and this acting."

—Dietrich Bonhoeffer[1]

" . . . the bosom of Mother Earth is in some way the bosom of God."

—Teilhard de Chardin[2]

[1] Dietrich Bonhoeffer, *Letters and Papers from Prison*, ed. E. Bethge (London: S. C. M. Press, 1971), p. 300.

[2] Teilhard de Chardin, *The Prayer of the Universe: Selected from Writings in Time of War*, trans. Rene Hague (London: Collins, Fontana Books, 1968), pp. 94–95.

Contents

Acknowledgments

*A*s with most human accomplishments, this book owes its existence and most of its best insights to a great number of other persons. Included in this list are my unforgettable teachers at Union Theological Seminary in New York City between 1953 and 1960, who taught me most of what I know, biblically and theologically, about the subject of prayer; and two remarkable women, Helen and Mary A. Kilborne, late of Orange, New Jersey, who lived prayer as I have tried here to write about it. The book also incorporates the gleanings of many conversations with my students, colleagues, and friends, to one of whom it is dedicated; and, needless to say, it reflects in both open and hidden ways my ongoing dialogue with the five other human beings who share my life most intimately, Rhoda and our four children.

Pausing to consider the above paragraph, I am struck by the fact that so many of the persons I have mentioned in it, explicitly by name or implied in the more general references, are women. I suspect this is not accidental. The fact that our mentors in prayer have often been women in itself speaks volumes. I am reminded of a sentence from a 1972 article by Anne McGrew Bennett (one of the women alluded to above, for she was part of the Union Seminary community acknowledged there). "One clergyman," she says, "wrote that he made it a point to attend women's missionary prayer meetings 'because you never could tell what women might take to praying about if left alone.'"* I am particularly indebted to Dr. Owen D. Owens of National Ministries of the American Baptist Churches, who persuaded me to elaborate in print some ideas that I had offered on this subject at a prayer conference in Columbus, Ohio, in 1984; and to Judson Press for inviting me to write this book.

Douglas John Hall

"Unter den Eichen"
Mitchell Island, Lake Huron
August 1986

---

*"Women in the New Society," in the *Journal of Current Social Issues,* United Church Board for Homeland Ministries, New York City, Vol. 11, No. 1, Winter 1972-73.

Introduction

Through Jesus Christ, Our Lord

"But who do you say that I am?" (Matthew 16:15).

What Is Prayer?

This is not a book about the mechanics of prayer. Others can speak more authoritatively than I on the subject of how to pray. There are important things to be said about that subject, but I am not the one to say them. On the whole, I suspect that the best sort of answer to the how-to aspect of our topic is the one offered by Karl Barth when he wrote, "How ought we to pray? It is not by chance that Jesus has given in the 'Our Father' a formula to teach [us] how to pray aright."[1]

My concern here is more elementary. I want to attempt to answer the questions What is prayer? What are we doing when we pray? Or perhaps it would be better to ask, What ought we to be doing when we pray? For the truth is, of course, that the term "prayer" connotes a great many things, and not all of them, as I shall hope to show in one of the chapters of this book, can be endorsed by thinking Christians.

Some people, for instance, seem to regard prayer chiefly as a means of self-improvement. They develop prayer habits and create worship opportunities in much the same way as others among our contemporaries cultivate physical exercise or aerobic dance—with a view to becoming more fulfilled, acceptable, interesting, beautiful, psychically stable, integrated, irenic, healthy, happy, satisfied, or positive people. One ventures to guess, in fact, that two-thirds of the literature written on the subject of prayer is addressed to precisely this type of motivation, books being, like everything else, determined by supply and demand.

But however natural and even to some extent Christian a thing it may be to wish to achieve some of the personal goals enumerated in the above list, those who take up the way of the cross can hardly be content with a view of prayer that makes the self the center and end of the entire process. It is to be hoped that those who pray in the name of Jesus Christ and follow where his Spirit leads may, in the last analysis, be changed for the better. But that is one of prayer's by-products, not its chief end. Self-improvement of whatever kind is a poor sort of motive for disciples of the One whose whole mission was to turn human beings away from preoccupation with self and towards God and neighbor.

The Preliminary Question

The tenor of the preceding section will, I hope, have introduced the reader to what is the primary presupposition of this brief study—namely, the assumption that we are to consider the subject of prayer as Christians, as persons for whom the basic meaning of any subject whatsoever, prayer included, is to be sought in contemplation of the events that form the foundational core of the gospel. We are not reflecting on the nature of prayer as a general human phenomenon that can be observed in every time and place, culture and cult, and even in societies like our own, which many would describe as being post-religious. We are not to consider prayer sociologically, psychologically, philosophically, or historically.

We are to ask about the meaning of prayer as this meaning is disclosed to us in faith under the impact of the Good News concerning Jesus, whom the church acknowledges to be the Christ.

To ask "What is prayer?" is to submit ourselves once more to the still more rudimentary question of our faith tradition: Who is Jesus Christ? What was and is transpiring in and through this One who stands at the center of our confession? As with every other subject to which Christians address themselves, the foundational material without which we could not construct our thought in any coherent manner is inseparably tied to the mystery at the heart of the Christian profession of faith, the mystery to which Paul gave expression in his introduction to the first letter to the church at Corinth: ". . . we preach Christ crucified. . ." (1 Corinthians 1:23).

This is, of course, not the place to undertake an elaborate discussion of the meaning of Jesus Christ's person and work. At the same time, neither can we circumvent all Christological and soteriological discussion and launch immediately into the subject of prayer; for all Christian prayer is through Jesus Christ, our Lord. What we think about Jesus Christ will color everything that we think about prayer. What we believe concerning the saving work of the Christ will influence every aspect of our conception of the meaning of prayer. If our thinking about the Christ is confused or only half-formed, our theology of prayer will certainly reflect this inadequacy in the foundations of our belief.

The previous sentence should not be construed to imply that anyone's understanding of Jesus Christ is ever truly adequate. No one who is honest and appropriately modest in relation to the mystery signified by this name will ever lay claim to the possession of a fully satisfying answer to the question that Jesus puts to his disciples in the quotation that stands at the head of this introduction, "But who do you say that I am?" Such a boast would be the ultimate vanity in both senses of the word "vanity." But every Christian, whether minister or layperson, whether highly educated in the subtleties of theology or professionally untutored, must have some image of Jesus and some guiding sense of who it is that he or she has promised to follow. It is this basic "picture of Christ" (*imago Christi*) about which we need to think as the prelude to our whole exercise. Who is Jesus and what was and is God doing through him? Our answer to the question that is the main topic of this essay (What is prayer?) will depend almost totally on the response that we make to this preliminary, Christological question.

Four Prominent Images of the Christ

There are, as can be observed very readily in the various patterns of Christianity at work in North American society today, a great many different ways of picturing Jesus, who he is, and what he intends for us. Each of these ways of seeing Jesus (John 12:21) leads to a certain corresponding conception of the character of the prayer that is undertaken in his name. Among the many actual possibilities, we shall consider four prominent images of the Christ together with the types of prayer theology to which they lead.

The Divine Jesus

For many persons in our society, among whom we find those who are often regarded as the most earnest of Christians, the dominant aspect of the person of Jesus is his divine origin and destiny. While these believers by no means reject or (necessarily) minimize the teachings of Jesus, his compassion as healer, his prophetic denunciations of religious and civil practices, or his suffering and death on the cross, what impresses them most in the whole presentation of the Christ in our tradition is his divinity. Unlike Adam, unlike all of us, Jesus is "the Son of God—"begotten, not made"— as the Nicene Creed formulated the matter. We are finite; Jesus is infinite ("Before Abraham was, I am."—John 8:58). We are sinful; Jesus was sinless (". . . in every respect tempted as we are, yet without sinning"—Hebrews 4:15). We are mortal; Jesus, though he assumed mortality, was and is immortal, the very Word (Logos) of God, who "was with God" and "was God" from eternity (John 1:1).

In short, the essential thing about Jesus for this particular faith posture is his participation in deity. It is not his humanity, but his divinity that is what ought to form the central focus of our belief, our discipleship, our worship, and all that we do. That the divine Logos "became flesh and dwelt among us" (John 1:14) is, of course, important for those holding to this viewpoint—though (as we shall see later) it is and always has been extremely tempting for Christians who are primarily excited by the thought of the wondrous divinity of the Christ to treat his humanity as a kind of formality. It is something to be suffered, so to speak, in order that the essential thing, namely his divine nature, might be manifested. No doubt the one who was "the first born of all creation" (Colossians 1:15), the second person of the holy Trinity, had to be "born in the likeness of men" (Philippians 2:7), for otherwise human beings could never know him or the truth that he imparts. The prophets and lawgivers of Israel had tried for centuries to bear witness to that truth; but finally only God "himself," God-come-among-us, could make it known.[2]

If this position answers the question of Jesus' identity by focusing on his divinity, its response to the soteriological side of the Christological question ("What has he done for us?") usually follows suit: what Jesus has done and continues to do for all who believe in him is that he takes them up into—incorporates them into—his divinity. Salvation thus means that I, being human, mortal, finite, and sinful, am given in Christ a new identity and a new and glorious future. While my old, corrupt self may continue to raise its persistent head above the waters of baptism, the new, "incorruptible" (1 Corinthians 15:52) self that is God's gift is being formed within me. While my "flesh" cannot "inherit the kingdom of God" (1 Corinthians 15:50), I shall at last be delivered from "this body of death" (Romans 7:24) and become a full participant in Christ's victory over all that sinful flesh is heir to.

Given such an orientation to the Christological basics of our tradition, it follows that prayer, within the circles formed around such an orientation, is chiefly a spiritual activity and discipline through which the faithful exercise their grace-given identity with the immortal Redeemer. In prayer, the believer seeks more fully to realize his or her incorporation into the "body of Christ," the church. Prayer is the soul's mode of "putting on" Christ (Galatians 3:27) or "the new nature" (Ephesians 4:24; Colossians 3:10). One may pray for and about many things; but what is primarily taking place in the act of prayer, given this basic stance, is a growth in grace (sanctification) towards the new, reborn self that is given the believer as he or she appropriates the life that flows from this divine Source. Through purgation, illumination, and union—"the threefold ladder of classical devotional theology"[3]—the soul attains identification with Christ.

Now to some who may read these words it might seem not only foolhardy but even blasphemous to enter any sort of protest against such a position. Indeed, this position would be regarded as the quintessence of Christian faith by countless Christians; and, in documenting the position with numerous quotations from the New Testament, I have myself been acknowledging, implicitly, that it has prominent biblical support. Not only scripturally, but also historically as well, Christians have always been deeply moved by the thought of the divine Christ who through baptism and Eucharist, through the Spirit, through the life of prayer and meditation, absorbs us into his divinity. "God became human," said Athanasius, summing up this point of view in a formula to which Christians have again and again resorted, "in order that we might become divine."[4] Who could object to such a venerable dogma?

It is not, of course, necessary to object to everything about a point of view in order to be critical of its fundamental assumptions or the direction in which it leads. No one who honors the authority of the Scriptures—least of all Protestants who hold to the *sola scriptura* (by Scripture alone) of the Reformation—would want to dispense with the language of the Christ's divinity, our incorporation into his Body, or prayer as the realization and sanctification of this new identity. Nor would any Christian who respects the long and impressive tradition of the church wish to dispense with Athanasius and all the others who have given to this position an authoritative and coherent definition. Yet there is, I believe, something quite misleading about this orientation as a faith posture. That assessment may be dismissed as a purely personal bias, yet I do not think that it can be so easily written off. There is, in the doctrinal position to which we have been alluding, what appears to be a rudimentary contradiction of the biblical orientation.

Since this study in its entirety concerns what I regard the biblical orientation to be, I shall not at this point attempt to elaborate extensively. This much, however, must already be stated: The whole movement of divine grace as it is presented in the continuity of the two testaments is towards creation not away from it. Redemption is not the overcoming of creation but the overcoming of that which has overcome creation. From the outset—quite literally from the first words of Genesis onwards—the God of the Scriptures is turned towards this world. Even the last book of the Christian Scriptures, Revelation, apocalyptic and devastating as it is in its judgment of what this world has become, sustains the creation-centeredness of biblical religion in general. The new heaven and new earth of which it speaks (Revelation 21:1) may indeed be new. Certainly it is not just the unfolding of natural historical possibilities; but neither is it entirely discontinuous with what God began eons before. What else has God intended from the beginning if not the very thing announced (proleptically) as completed at last in Revelation 21:3 and following?

. . .and I heard a great voice from the throne saying, "Behold, the dwelling of God is with men. He will dwell with them, and they shall be his people, and God himself will be with them; he will wipe away every tear from their eyes, and death shall be no more, neither shall there be mourning nor crying nor pain any more, for the former things have passed away."

Above all, this orientation of the divine towards the created, the human, the historical, is underscored by the incarnation, humiliation, and glorification of God's Word. Unlike other ancient religions of dying and rising gods, which accent the deification of those who achieve mystical identification with the god, the story of

"Jesus Christ and him crucified" (1 Corinthians 2:2) is primarily about our humanization. He became human in order that we might become truly human. The gospel may even be described (as no less orthodox a theologian than Barth has described it)[5] as having for its basic subject the "humanity" of God: God, who all the way through this story told in the chronicles of Israel yearns with an unquenchable pathos for communion with the creature; God who finally cannot resist the parental longing and moves, at infinite cost, into complete proximity with prodigal humanity.

Given such an orientation, any religion that has the end effect of translating human beings out of the world God made must be called into question. That religion may use a great deal of the language of biblical faith. It may present itself in its host culture as impressively spiritual, sincere, and pious. It may be able to achieve the reputation of real Christianity, thus distinguishing itself from all the halfhearted bourgeois religion and thinly disguised humanism with which, characteristically, it contrasts its own true belief. It may also produce the most fervent forms of prayer. But if, all the while, its real effect is to turn human beings away from the earth and towards some heaven, how will it square itself with the One who "so loved the world?"

The Conquering Jesus

Sometimes the religious fascination with our Lord's divinity combines with the more political idea of divine sovereignty to produce a picture of Jesus as conqueror. As a child in Sunday school, I remember, I was occasionally obliged to sing a hymn whose opening line announced, "O the world must be conquered for Christ." I no longer recall the words that followed, but the tune is indelibly fixed in my mind. It is stirring and military. The truth is, a great deal of Christian art and imagery throughout the ages has been essentially military in character—which seems an odd sort of fate for the one called "Prince of Peace."

While the mentality that fastens upon the divine Jesus lures the human spirit away from this world, the concept of Jesus as conqueror moves the faithful towards the world—with militant intent! Jesus is depicted as the Victor, the Captain, the King. He has already fought the decisive battle. In principle, at least, "the enemy" has been vanquished. Who is the enemy? In classical expressions of this Christology, the enemy is Satan, or Death, or Sin: transcendent "powers and principalities" (see Ephesians 6:12). But in practice it has always been hard for the church as it was moved by this particular conception of its Head to separate these otherworldly enemies or (in the case of Sin) personifications of human conditions that apply, after all, to every one of us, from quite specific earthly enemies: the infidel, the heathen, the unbeliever, the Turk, and the Jew. An imperial Christianity possessed of the thought that Jesus wants to complete the victory over his enemies, which he has already in principle effected in the resurrection and ascension to power, is a force to be reckoned with. History bears stunning testimony to the fact.

It is not only a thing of the past. This ancient, Christocratic ideal is still very much with us. Possibly it is even stronger than ever—at least on this continent. For the power of this ideal is and always has been directly related to the strength of the empires with which is has been associated; and the United States is perhaps the strongest empire ever. The combination of triumphalistic religion and imperialistic politics can be extremely provocative. If the religious concept of the conquering Christ is a heady one, it is all the more exhilarating when combined at the political level with a vigorous "Christian" empire. The obvious material power and glory of the empire give concreteness to the religious ideal, while the latter lends to the empire its sense of divine mandate and approval, something the empire always craves. From Constantine onwards, the Christology that depicted Jesus in the role of warrior-prince has been attracted to the empire as its natural political parallel. The attraction has been mutual. "In this sign conquer" (*in hoc signo vinces*) is what the emperor Constantine is said to have seen written over the Chi-Rho symbol in his famous dream before the battle of the Milvian bridge, where he did indeed conquer; and ever since then, "Christian" nations, finding themselves drawn into the seductive vortex of imperialism, have discovered the usefulness of a Christ so conceived.

For one thing, every empire needs its enemies. Without an enemy to whom continuous attention can be paid, too much public notice is drawn to the internal problems and flaws of the imperium itself. Part of the usefulness of a Christ figure who conquers is that he can help to persuade people that the enemies of the empire are the enemies of God. They must be conquered, vanquished, destroyed, not only in the name of some political theory (democracy, free enterprise, and so forth) but also in the name of God, of Jesus Christ, and of all that is sacred. They are not only a threat to a "way of life" (the American way, for instance); they are a threat to life as God intended it. (Is this not what many of our fellow citizens have in mind when they speak about "the Communists" or "the Russians"?)

If Jesus is conqueror, and if what he does for us is to conquer our enemies (including our internal enemies—the human lusts and passions), then prayer is primarily a discipline through which we submit ourselves to our captain and are trained up as soldiers for the battle. (Now I remember the chorus of that Sunday school hymn. It went, "Forward, soldiers!" Forward, soldiers! To the war in the name of the Lord!"

"Discipline" is the key word here. Prayer is a discipline. Actually, the term "discipline" is a perfectly good theological word, coming from the same root as disciple: *discere,* to learn. But like many good words of the faith, the word "discipline" is thoroughly colored by its long association with the pedagogical methods by which people were supposed to have been equipped to "discern" the truth, including rote memorization of Scriptures, stern catechismal practices, vigilant and humorless ministers and elders, and so forth. It happens, in consequence, that for a considerable number of our contemporaries the discipline of prayer is an extremely unattractive proposition. It conjures up images of a kind of psychic flagellation, a scourging of all the excuses and diversions and entertainments that keep us from being really earnest and ready "soldiers of Christ," a spiritual regimentation equipping us to go out dutifully and do our part in "conquering the world for Christ."

But besides its lack of appeal to all who seek joy in life—and more important theologically—this image of the Christ and the theology of prayer that it engenders begs questions that sensitive human beings living in a pluralistic society like ours can hardly ignore. Is it really the will of God that the whole inhabited earth should become Christian? If so, then Christian according to whom, or what? The dominant patterns of Christian societies past and present do not evoke universal admiration, to say the least. Did Jesus really have in mind something comparable to the Holy Roman Empire or any other empire when he spoke about his "kingdom"? "My kingdom* is not of this world," he said to the official representative of the Roman imperium, by whom he was being tried. He added, ". . . *if* my kingship were of this world, my servants would fight, that I might not be handed over. . . ; but my kingship is not from the world" (John 18:36). When Pilate then cleverly noted that Jesus seemed, all the same, ready to accept the appellation "king," Jesus said something about the sovereignty of truth. Some, with Pilate, would judge that his words were rather ineffectual; but do they not contain, in fact, the essential critique of this whole Christology?

For it makes a good deal of difference, so far as the attitudes and the ethic that it produces are concerned, if instead of claiming the triumph of "my" Christ I think of Christian discipleship in terms of the ongoing discernment of a conquering "truth." What wins, in that case, is not this or that Christology, and not Christianity, and not the church, but the truth to which (by grace alone!) some Christology, some Christians, and some churches now and then may clumsily point, but which is by no means bottled up in any of them. What conquers is not Christian ideologies or Christian armies. What is conquered is not infidels or atheists or members of other religious traditions. What is victorious is the truth that Jesus lived and was (John 14:6), and what is overcome by this ongoing victory is falsehood and bluster and inauthenticity wherever they are found—beginning, as the First Epistle of Peter would have it, with "the household of God"! (1 Peter 4:17).

In other words, as with the previous misleading image of Jesus, we do not have to abandon all the concepts and symbols that are associated with this picture of the Christ. We do not have to eschew altogether the idea of victory in our thinking about the foundational events of the gospel. But we do, I think, have to get over the centuries-old habit of casting Jesus in the role of a military potentate, thus giving to God what only belongs to Caesar, if it belongs to anyone at all. Prayer that forms itself around the quest for discernment of the truth that Jesus was and is will be a very different kind of discipline from the prayer that equips little children to go out to "war in the name of the Lord."

The Judging Jesus

One image of the Christ that powerfully sways our society calls us to abandon the world, another to take it over. But there is a still more ominous *imago Christi* at work in our midst; and it is that of an angry Jesus who is about to destroy a world that is no longer, if it ever was, redeemable. Redemption there is, according to this posture, for "the elect." These few will be taken into consummate fellowship with the Lord just before the final cataclysm. For them, the end of the world will be the Rapture. But for the vast majority of human beings (and as we may add, symbolically, with the author of Jonah [in 4:11] for "much cattle"), the end will just be the bitter end.

After a brief season of respite from such wrath, the judging Jesus has again become very popular in our time. No doubt it has something to do with the law-and-order backlash, and with the approach of the apocalyptic-sounding year 2000. But whatever may be the cause of its present popularity, the picture of Christ as implacable judge is by no means novel.

Like the two previous types of answer to the question, "But

who do you say that I am?" this answer can also command a certain biblical basis. Judgment, as even an occasional reader of the Bible knows, belongs to the Judeo-Christian tradition. In fact, God as judge can be met on every page of the Bible, even where there is no explicit reference to this particular attribute of the divine Person. God judges the world because, as Creator, God has some definitive intention for creation. When this intention is thwarted, as it regularly is by willful human beings and societies, then God expresses the sorrow, disappointment, anger, and even wrath that we mean when we speak about divine judgment. This judgment is in fact the foundation of the Law and the Prophets. The law of God is given as "a lamp unto my feet" (Psalm 119:105), so that I may understand God's intention for history, and, through obedience, both foster that intention and avoid God's judgment of those who willfully or inadvertently obstruct God's purposes. The prophets are those persons whose special vocation and burden it is to be made unusually sensitive to what God is doing in the world and, therefore, particularly conscious as well of human disregard of and disrespect for God's mysterious ways. It would be unthinkable, therefore, for a faith tradition founded upon the religious experience of the people of Israel—as Christianity is—to end with a Messiah who knows nothing of judgment. Christ the judge is a necessary and entirely consistent consequence of the New Testament's faithful adherence to the basic theistic principles of the older Scriptures. It was biblically and theologically unconvincing and ethically irresponsible when the sentimental Liberalism of some nineteenth- and early twentieth-century Christians presented the world with a meek and mild Jesus from whom the dimension of judgment had been removed.

But while judgment is thus a rudimentary element of biblical faith generally and of the Christ of the Gospels and Epistles in particular, it is a far cry from this recognition to the type of religious mentality that seems capable of entertaining salvation only in company with the thought of the world's imminent destruction. In the preceding paragraph I used a certain word in describing God's judgment that is extremely important for a genuine understanding of the biblical concept of divine judgment. Not that the word as such is important, but what it means is vastly significant, and I seldom find this nuance to be present in the witness of those Christians who insist on presenting Jesus first of all as this world's wrathful judge. I am referring to the idea of divine sorrow—*pathos*, to use the more technical term. In his impressive work on prophecy, Abraham Heschel has claimed that pathos is the essence of the prophets' conception of God.[6] When God's intention for the world is frustrated, I wrote, then God expresses the sorrow, disappointment, anger, and even wrath that we mean when we speak of divine judgment.

It is this same holy sorrow that very often shows through poignantly, in the Gospel pictures of Jesus: Jesus who would gather Jerusalem as a hen gathers her chicks (Matthew 23:37; Luke 13:34); Jesus who wept at the untimely death of his friend Lazarus (John 11:35); Jesus whose "sweat became like great drops of blood falling down upon the ground" as he prayed for humankind in the garden of sorrows (Luke 22:44); Jesus who refused to pray for power (Matthew 26:53), but continued his ministry of healing (Luke 22:51) even in the face of his own arrest and violent death.

The New Testament's handling of this theme goes well beyond Jesus' personal exemplification of the dimension of sorrow that informs it from the beginning. It presents the Christ as the one who, finally, must himself bear the consequences of the judgment that he announces. "He was bruised for our iniquities . . ." (Isaiah 53:5). The substitutionary Christology of Western Christian tradition may have many flaws, but in this at least it captures the essence of the biblical resolution of God's ancient struggle between judgment and mercy: namely, that the cost of this resolution must be borne by God's own person, represented in the Anointed One, the Messiah. As Christians we must stand in the environs of Golgotha, as Karl Barth often put it; but we are not called to bear the unbearable consequences of our own distortions of our creaturehood and of creation.

To present Jesus as the judge who brings about salvation only through destruction and damnation is to ignore this whole dimension of the gospel—which is in fact no "dimension," but the central core of the whole Christian message. The grace of God, as Bonhoeffer insisted, is by no means cheap.[7] Our wholeness is acquired at great cost. But the greatest cost is borne, not by the world, not by us, but by God alone. Through hearing, through baptism and Eucharist, through the continuing baptism of the Holy Spirit who brings the church into solidarity with God's worldly sorrow and suffering, and through prayer, we are brought close enough to the divine *krisis* (judgment) to know that our condition is indeed critical—that we are unworthy of love and mercy, that we are acceptable only "by grace . . . through faith" (Ephesians 2:8). But the end of the matter, as it was spelled out in all the major expressions of Reformation thought, is not the "satisfaction" of God's righteousness. The end of the matter is the righting of God's world. The making right (justification) of the fallen creature is (for the Reformers) the meaning of the righteousness of God.

When prayer is informed by the picture of a Christ whose judgment is the goal of his appearing, it is rather predictable what prayer will then connote. What it in fact does connote for perhaps millions of people in North America today is the means—or one of the primary means—whereby they hope to escape judgment, in particular the Last Judgment. Or, positively stated, prayer is the medium through which they can ensure their personal participation in the company of those who shall experience the Rapture. They see these as the final days of planet Earth, and therefore their object, in all that they do, is to prepare for the end and for the real life that can be attained only on the far side of earth's annihilation.

In introducing this picture of the Christ, I used the word "ominous." I do not think it inappropriate to resort to such a strong term in this connection. When a significant portion of the population of the world's most powerful nation starts believing in the imminent end of the world, and even praying for it, it is not likely that they will provide many reasons why this world should not be terminated—to put it in the most charitable manner I can devise. In such a world as ours, whose continued existence depends upon our human resourcefulness in providing reasons "to be," and whose annihilation is almost assured unless such reasons can be continuously and imaginatively propagated, an attitude of this nature is ominous. Between those who use Christ to help them escape the world, those who expect him to assist them in conquering it, and those last who pray for its speedy termination, the Christian movement today seems often, to the sensitive, a less-than-trustworthy friend of the Earth.

But perhaps the readers of this book will not be able to identify themselves wholly with any of these three ways of picturing the One through whom Christians pray. I suspect they will not. In that case, we should turn now to a fourth image of the Christ; one more likely, unless I am mistaken, to speak to readers of this book.

The Accepting Jesus

The hymn "Jesus Loves Me" ("Jesus loves me, this I know; for the Bible tells me so") captures immediately and sympathetically the basic Christological mood of most of us who continue, despite ongoing migrations, to adhere to the old Protestant denominations of the Western world. Not everyone means the same thing when they sing this familiar children's hymn. There are sophisticated and also very simple backgrounds of spiritual reflection brought to the singing and hearing of such a hymn. However, it is by no means only the child or the simple believer who is able to identify with the sentiments of this poem by Anna Bartlett Warner. When the great Barth visited the United States in 1962 and was asked by a rather bold student of theology what, after all these years of study and contemplation, he felt that he had learned, the seventy-six-year-old Swiss theologian answered (with a characteristic twinkle), "Jesus loves me, this I know; for the Bible tells me so."

For both liberal Christianity (in the broadest sense of the term "liberal") and the more orthodox or neo-orthodox forms of classical Protestantism, what is essential about Jesus is his embodiment and exemplification of the divine love—*agape*, that "spontaneous and unmotivated"[8] love of which John writes in chapter 3 verse 16, which Paul so beautifully characterizes in 1 Corinthians 13, which informed the whole outlook of Peter Abelard when he asked about the meaning of the death of Christ, and which Anna Bartlett Warner set to poetry in her little song. It is this love, this selfless and sacrificial giving and not counting the cost, that ordinary Christians remember when all the doctors of theology have had their say about paradox and original sin and atonement. Sometimes even the doctors of theology are caused to remember this above all.

Yet truly simple things are never just simple. "Seek simplicity," quipped Alfred North Whitehead, "and distrust it." I do not think he meant that simplicity is as such untrustworthy, but rather that what we human beings do with simple things is often very questionable. What we do is that we simplify: that is, we take profound and ineffable truth—truth, for instance, like that contained in the straightforward statement that "Jesus loves me"—and we turn it into a singing commercial. We sloganize precisely to avoid the depth of mystery and judgment that is glimpsed through the prism of such an unadorned declaration of God's unthinkable love; precisely in order to evade the questioning, the contemplation of past and future, the confrontation with Self and Other that is tucked away in this declaration; precisely so that we may return as quickly as possible to our routine and ordered lives, where mystery is no more unsettling than an Agatha Christie detective story. We regularly make simple things simplistic. We pick up Aladdin's lamp and call it a conversation piece. We make the Bible, which according to statistics is found in 95 percent of American homes, part of our decor.

Sloganized, domesticated, thoroughly housebroken, "Jesus loves me" becomes: Jesus likes me, accepts me, and makes no great demands upon me. Jesus loves me, and loves us, just as we are.

Of course we aren't perfect—who is? But basically, we are okay. When all is said and done, we are good people. A popular book about suffering is entitled, *When Bad Things Happen to Good People.*[9] The book has much to commend itself to all of us who are inheritors of the Judeo-Christian tradition. It makes some very important and very helpful points about suffering. But one wonders, reading it, how many of the thousands who seek comfort from this book ever question seriously whether they are in fact "good" people to whom "bad things" have happened or may happen. "Why do you ask me about what is good?" demanded Jesus of the one who thought that eternal life could be purchased with good deeds. "One there is who is good" (Matthew 19:17). All our goodness is tainted—"all our righteous deeds are like a polluted garment" (Isaiah 64:6).

There are, of course, times and places where the only appropriate translation of the Christian message is a word of sheer, unconditional acceptance. What many people consider Paul Tillich's greatest sermon was entitled "You Are Accepted."[10] It was written as a contemporary rendition of the meaning of the Protestant Reformation's central principle, justification by grace through faith; and at the edge of the manuscript, Tillich, who had just become sixty, wrote, "For myself." For he knew (what all who possess real self-knowledge know) that he was not, simply, "acceptable."

However, it is just this preliminary self-knowledge—the awareness of our fundamental unloveliness and unrighteousness— that prevents the declaration that Jesus loves and accepts us from becoming misleading and simplistic. Unfortunately, there seems all too little hard evidence that most human beings of middle-class station in our society are ready to face all that.

I inserted the phrase "of middle-class station" in that sentence, not only because that is in fact the socio-economic status of most of us who have membership in what we are still pleased to call the "mainline" denominations, but also because it is necessary to view this picture of Jesus as the accepting Christ from a corporate as well as an individual perspective. Perhaps where individual persons are concerned, each with her or his little tragedies and impossibilities, the Christian gospel must always have about it a quality of unconditional acceptance. Yet we are never just individual persons, we are members of societies, cultures, worlds. It is one thing for the rich individual, knowing (what Dives failed to recognize in Luke 16:19-31) his ultimate poverty, to say, "Jesus loves me." But does Jesus simply love and accept us rich people of the so-called First World? Is Jesus ready to condone the injustice, oppression, and violence that is, apparently, an inevitable consequence of our world's need to sustain and foster its being first? Even of us as individuals, our personal sorrows and vulnerability notwithstanding, must it not be asked whether Jesus loves us just as we are, with our ambitions, our material acquisitiveness, our drives for power, recognition, and popular acceptance all intact?

Those who regard the One at the center of Christian belief and confession as the great Affirmer and Accepter of persons pray accordingly: they pray that they will believe in their being loved; that they will accept the reality of their acceptance. No wonder! It is never easy for human beings of integrity to believe that they are accepted. Even the affirmation of love on the part of another human being is hard for us really to trust. Like young lovers, we are always in need of being told repeatedly that we are loved. How much more is this the case where the affirmation of God's love is concerned! It is not surprising that millions of middle-class North Americans still show up in their churches every Sunday, their skepticism about God notwithstanding, and wait to be reassured once more that Jesus loves them. The need is exacerbated by the fact that, in the meantime, the rest of the world has been announcing with increasing regularity that it does not much love these same North Americans!

Who is callous enough to make light of this very human need? Jesus did not scorn the sincere longing of the rich young ruler for acceptance and affirmation (Luke 18:18-25). Yet the prophetic tradition, to which Jesus belonged, could not simply give in to the pathos of individual lives caught in the web of socioeconomic destinies greater than their own willing. "I am a man of unclean lips," confessed the prophet Isaiah in the presence of the holy One, "and I dwell in the midst of a people of unclean lips" (Isaiah 6:5). There are things about us that are in fact quite unacceptable to the holy and just God of our faith. To portray Jesus exclusively as the Affirmer and Accepter of us and of me is to turn a blind eye to those unacceptable things. What is worse, it is to turn a blind eye to the persons of the whole world (the Third World especially) whose existence is profoundly affected by what is wrong with us. When, under the impact of such a Christology, prayer focuses on acceptance (self-acceptance, social acceptance, acceptance of what is, of the status quo), then Christian faith is robbed of that entire quality that is signified by the biblical word *metanoia*, meaning "repentance, change, turning about."

The Transforming Christ

We have noticed, then, how four fairly typical images of the central figure of our faith give rise to differing conceptions of the nature and function of prayer in the Christian life. We have seen that each of these pictures of Christ produces a conception of prayer that contains misleading elements—elements that must be assessed critically, not because of an arbitrary precommitment to some alternative theory, but because they appear to distort or obscure certain central emphases of the gospel.

In each case, it is in its attitude towards the world that this distortion manifests itself most conspicuously. The first approach encourages world denial and evasion of creaturely responsibility; the second a triumphalistic bid for worldly power; the third outright rejection of the created order; and the fourth an uncritical acceptance of the status quo. Prayer, in each of these approaches to the life of faith in Christ, is a potent spiritual conditioner in the formation of people's attitudes towards their world. When persons pray under the influence of one or another of these images of the one through whom they are praying, they not only construct and reinforce their particular picture of the divine source and ground of life, but they articulate and, over the years, consolidate an orientation towards this world which—in my view, at any rate—must be seriously questioned from the perspective of the gospel concerning "Jesus Christ and him crucified" (1 Corinthians 2:2).

Of course, this assertion obliges me to say, at last, what I should want to answer to the question that is quoted at the beginning of this introduction. It will be obvious that in all the foregoing discussion I have been assuming such an answer—I hope a more or less consistent one. In fact, my purpose in characterizing these four positions (and perhaps for that reason I have overstated them) has been, primarily, to prepare myself and my readers for a statement of my own response to the question that Jesus put to his disciples at Caesarea Philippi, and that he puts to all of us. (It is a well-seasoned way of doing theology. The medieval theologians called it *via negativa* [by way of negation]: you approach your own position, gradually, by "negating" other actual or hypothetical positions.)

In negating the four approaches above (not everything they stand for, but their basic thrusts), I have implied, all along, certain positive affirmations concerning the Christ and the life of prayer into which we are beckoned when, daily, we take his yoke and his burden upon us. Thus, in rejecting the divine Jesus who calls human beings away from things temporal and earthly and fixes their gaze on the eternal, I have been maintaining that the movement of God in Christ is towards this world, not away from it. Consequently, those who are moved by the gospel of the crucified One will, like Peter of the *Quo Vadis* legend,[11] find their personal and no doubt understandable desire to escape the often horrendous realities of this world hindered by a Spirit that turns them back into the world to suffer with it and for it, as their Lord did. The fact that this worldly Christ and his followers suffer in the world should deter anyone who is tempted to construe what I am maintaining here as if it were a case of accomodation. Neither the Christ nor those who follow him in obedience are *of* the world. But they are certainly in the world; and I should say that faith, in the Christian sense, is nothing more nor less than the God-given courage to be in the world intentionally and without reserve.

However, we are not here as conquerors. In eliminating the image of Christ as conqueror, I have been insisting by implication that Jesus is first of all servant: ". . . I am among you as one who serves" (Luke 22:27). It is not accidental that the faith of the early church quickly made the connection between Christ crucified and Isaiah's Suffering Servant. If Jesus is also Lord, Master, and King (and clearly the church regarded him so from the beginning), it requires nothing less than a transvaluation of values (a radical redefinition of terms) to make such titles fit his story as it is recorded in the Gospels. What sort of master suffers the insults, downright stupidity, and final disloyalty of his own followers? What manner of king rides into his imperial city on a donkey? Kings ride horses, or go about in bulletproof vehicles. What kind of lord washes the feet of his subjects? Even to begin to comprehend what the lordship of Jesus Christ means, we have to unlearn all that we have been taught to understand by terms like "dominion," "domination," "dominant," and most of the other terms having to do with power and sovereignty. In this strange, new[12] biblical landscape, mastery means service and strength is weakness and the meek, not the aggressive, are the inheritors of the earth. Jesus the Servant-Lord, the Victor who is Victim, calls into existence a community of service, a people willing to sacrifice their own well-being for the well-being of others, especially the world's victims. Only in this respect is it permitted for Christians to speak about "overcoming"the world [we shall overcome]. They are not called to overcome on their own behalf, or through force, numerical strength, violence, crusades, or the like, but only for others. They are to do this by means of a love that has cast out fear and learned to align itself with the oppressed, not with conquerors.

I reject the imagery of the angry, judging Christ—who like that fabled American officer in Vietnam thought that in order to save a village he would have to destroy it. I have in mind a different concept of the work of the Christ. My alternative picture of Jesus also contains the element of judgment, for, contrary again to the accepting Jesus of the fourth approach, I do not believe that everything is acceptable. But the judgment that must be part of any scripturally based Christology and soteriology is a means and not the end. The goal of the divine economy, so far as the whole tradition of Jerusalem is concerned, is life and not death, health (*salus*) and not sickness, mercy and not vindication, the righting of what is wrong and not obliteration. Those who today are depicting Jesus as the great Annihilator, ready to use nuclear holocaust to effect his plan of salvation, have confused Christ with Antichrist. They have apparently not heard that it is the thief in the night who comes to destroy, not the Good Shepherd. The Shepherd does not slaughter the sheep, but on the contrary lays down his own life for them (John 10:11). "For God sent the Son into the world, not to condemn the world, but that the world might be saved through him" (John 3:17).

At the same time, the opposite image of a Christ (which is partly, of course, a liberal reaction to the above), who only accepts what is there provides us with occasion to notice that there is a passion for justice in the love with which, in Jesus, God loves us. Therefore, there is judgment against everything that makes for worldly injustice. It is hard for the rich Christians of the Northern Hemisphere to enter God's kingdom. It is not impossible, however, for God is able to transform also the rich.

In our particular socio-historical context, what we need most of all to see when we think of Jesus is One who intends to transform the world. To transform something means to change its form, shape, direction; to turn it towards a different goal; to reorient it. Jesus does not want to take us out of the world, he wants to put us into it with a different vision (see John 17:15). Jesus does not intend that we conquer the world, but that we befriend it. Jesus certainly does not wish to gather about him a band of nihilists, ready to "push over what is falling" (Nietzsche's characterization of nihilism); he recruits only those who are committed, as he is, to creation's mending.[13] Jesus does not call into discipleship those who are unwilling to see that the world is radically in need of being mended; he intends us to see that what is there is not acceptable as it is but can be changed!

This transforming Christ calls us to participate in his transfiguration of creation. It is a work that can be accomplished only from within, and so it involves a kind of journey into the interior. To follow Jesus means to enter the life of the world in a way that none who have ever followed him conceived, at first, to be possible; for it leads into the very heart of the darkness, the broken heart of the world God made. Only from that place can the process of healing begin to occur.[14]

Such a journey is not altogether attractive to any of us. We know how to admire, from afar, the world healers—the Teresas and Dietrichs and Dags and Helders and Jeans. I am acquainted with a young Mennonite woman, a petite and fragile person just out of undergraduate studies, one of my own former students. Today she is one of four North Americans who live in a thousand-member refugee camp in El Salvador as "international presences" to discourage the death squads from performing their bloody office. I greatly admire such courage—from the safety of my chair of theology. But I know, all the same, that Jesus is requiring of all of us today that we come over to the side of life, the world's life, putting our frail minds and, if necessary, our even frailer bodies between human and creational survival and the ubiquitous death squads of a civilization gone awry.

And prayer? Well, if Jesus is really a transforming Presence who intends to turn us in love towards this luminous and threatened creation; to turn even us towards the dark interior of our world, despite our penchant for comfort and success and a painless life and death, then what can prayer be if not an ongoing, Spirit-initiated struggle to *think our way into God's world?*

That, in any case, is the basic thesis of this little book. The rest of it will have to try and demonstrate whether such an hypothesis is tenable, workable, and faithful. In the long run, of course, only the future of the Christian movement itself will decide that issue.

Finally, to provide some rudimentary guidance (purpose and nature) to the reader, let me comment very briefly on the structure of the book. It is divided into two parts. The first part addresses basic questions about the *purpose* of prayer; the second is concerned with the *nature* of prayer, and explicitly with the relation between praying and thinking. Each part is divided into four chapters, and I have kept the chapters rather brief and concentrated on one basic subject. In this way I have hoped not only to make the material more communicable, but also to facilitate group discussion; for I should like the book to lend itself to study and dialogue about the nature and purpose of prayer, both at the seminary and the congregational levels.

Escape Hatch
or Doorway
to Reality?

Part I

Chapter 1

Living with Marx's Question

"I do not pray that thou shouldst take them out of the world, but that thou shouldst keep them from the evil one" (John 17:15).

"Opiate of the People"

Despite persistent rumors of wild-eyed Christian Marxists toting guns and doctrinaire Communists disguised as Christian priests and ministers, there are in fact very few Christians who are prepared to describe themselves unqualifiedly as Marxists or Communists—though the tradition of Christian socialism is a very well-established one, claiming the adherence or respect of most of the "great" theologians of our epoch.[15]

But while Marxism as such is at many points incompatible with Christian belief (so is capitalism), Karl Marx and those who have interpreted his point of view in our century have many things to teach Christians about the meaning of their own gospel—partly, it must be admitted, because the biblical tradition and certain Reformation and other forms of Christianity constitute a goodly portion of the background of reflection, concern, and hope by which Marx and his followers were themselves deeply influenced. In a demonstrable way, the Marxist critique of class, property, and government is in a direct line of descent from the prophetic traditions of Israel and the church. Thus when one of the most perceptive Marxist philosophers of our time (who today, being *persona non grata* with the Czech State, plays the organ in a Roman Catholic church in Prague) asks whether sincere Marxists are not in some respects the real followers of Jesus in our age, Christians must at least be prepared to let such a question disturb their consciences.[16] The Jesus who described his true disciples, not as those who said the right words but performed the right acts might well recognize in Marxists and others, who take up the causes of their poor and oppressed neighbors, disciples more faithful to him than are many who announce themselves openly as Christians.

What concerns us here, however, is not Marx's social analysis but this critique of religion. As is well known, Karl Marx asserted that religion is "the opiate of the people."[17] He did not say opiate for the people—that was Lenin's interpretation of the matter. Lenin saw religion as something "laid on" from above, imposed and nurtured by the ruling classes in order to keep the masses in their place. Students of Christianity and other religions will not discount Lenin's explanation either. A glance at the role of religion in the maintenance of the institution of slavery, class divisions, sex roles, and so forth, ought to discourage a too hasty defense of any of the historic faiths. Yet Marx's formulation of the function of religion is, I think, more profound than Lenin's. Marx recognizes the deeply psychic need of religious belief. This need originates in the anxious spirit of *homo sapiens.* People do not grasp after God and heaven because some czar or group of entrepreneurs ordain it. Religion is not a capitalist plot, although capitalists have been able to employ to advantage the human thirst for the divine, and though many contemporary shareholders in multinational corporations would be glad enough if more of the workers in their industries were staunch and obedient Christians, content with their earthly lot while waiting for real life to begin afterwards. Marx knew, however, that the religious impulse is deeper than the various uses and abuses to which it can be and is put. It is bound up with the human need to endure in spite of the terrifying darkness and chaos that surrounds us and threatens always to engulf us.

The Terror of Existence

Human beings are, after all, extremely fragile and defenseless creatures. We do not know to what extent other creatures of God are open to the terror of existence; but we know all too well that we ourselves are exposed to untold dangers within and without. I am not referring only to the terrible fates that can overtake our bodies in a twinkling (the word "cancer" causes even strong and healthy persons to wince), nor even to the more public catastrophes—the natural disasters, environmental "accidents," the Third World War—of which we are reminded every time we turn on the television or pick up a newspaper. I do not even have in mind, in any exclusive sense, the debilitating psychic traumas that can be induced by personal tragedies, distorted human relationships, or far less dramatic causes. I mean, rather, that simply by being human, conscious, sensitive—simply by thinking about life—we court a whole spectrum of fears that can very easily overwhelm us. As every sensitive pastor knows, these fears take hold of ordinary people; they do not confine themselves to the conspicuously neurotic.

To illustrate: a young woman, characteristically bright and jovial, calls up and wants to discuss "something private" with her pastor. She arrives at his door, breathless and visibly embarrassed— but desperate. She and her husband have wanted a child, but they can't seem to "beget" one. Some time ago they decided to adopt. But yesterday afternoon she read "this article" about a mother in some American city—a sane woman who had suddenly "gone berserk" and strangled her baby. My God! She might do the same thing! Hadn't they better call off the adoption procedures?

This woman is by no means unique. In a way she is everyone. There is a darkness on the edge of our consciousness, and for most of us it takes a little more than a newspaper article with some hint of a parallel to our own situation to arouse our primordial apprehensiveness of that darkness. A great deal of the activity with which we busy ourselves is designed, subconsciously, to distract our overly curious minds from their dangerous fascination with that forbidden realm. Folk wisdom understood this long before Freud and Jung and other cartographers of the human psyche described it scientifically. That is why our language is dotted with proverbs and codified bits of advice for coping with our own internal demons: "The devil finds work for idle fingers," "Let sleeping dogs lie," "Cross your bridges when you come to them," and so forth.

The Comfort of Religion

What Marx meant by religion as the people's opiate was that religion is both the most common and the most effective way in which human beings seek to cope with their conscious and unconscious dismay at existence. Following Feuerbach, he considered the religious impulse a matter of "projection": proceeding from our own limitations, we project onto the invisible screen of eternity images of a source of security that enable us to live with our fears. We know that we are finite beings: we are "being-toward-death," as Heidegger phrased it. Unlike other finite beings, we are fully conscious of our finitude and of all our weaknesses. So we summon the courage to be through believing in an infinite and eternal Source, in whose transcendent being we may participate. We are weak creatures, limited in physical strength even when we are outwardly full of bravado and machismo (perhaps especially then), no match even for the larger or swifter animals let alone the immense natural forces of our environment. So we find comfort in the belief in an all-powerful force or deity whose omnipotence has befriended us and in whose strength we may have some portion. Again, we are—for all our knowledge—ignorant creatures. Our wisest ones know that they are not wise, that their knowledge represents an infinitely small and tentative aspect of what there is to be known—of what perhaps must be known if we are to survive as a species. So we confront the fact of our existential ignorance with the countervailing "fact" of an all-wise, omniscient deity, who has "revealed" to us what we could not know in and of ourselves, and whose ineffable wisdom, inaccessible to us in its fullness, is behind everything that happens—with the very satisfying consequence that we can believe that whatever happens always happens "for the best."

Why Religion Has to Be Eradicated

Marx was not snide about religion (although some Marxists are), because he knew the pathos of humanity out of which religion emerges. Anxious, faltering humankind can hardly be chastised for discovering ways of continuing in the face of external and internal realities that could easily reduce less inventive beings to self-destruction. (One wonders, in fact, whether the self-destruction that is being pursued so avidly by the nations today might not be traced to the demise of religious inventiveness—the "death of God.")

Yet while he was not superior in his attitude towards religion, Marx was all the same angry about is effects. The reason for his anger can be understood easily enough. To grasp something of its rationale, we need only return for a moment to the final sentence in the preceding subsection: an omniscient deity guides the whole process of history, claims the religious mentality, with an ineffable wisdom; and though we frail mortals cannot understand a good deal of what happens to and around us, we can be sure that it is all providential, all for the best.

The Marxist asks, "Is it really for the best?" Is it for the best when millions of children die of malnutrition in a world that has a glut of wheat? When in our cities the very rich live in proximity to the very poor, without even knowing it? When the people who labor are deprived of any of the just rewards of their labor by greedy industrialists? When mothers and little children are made to work for hours on end in airless mines and merciless, machine-serving factories (as was the case in Marx's Europe)?

One could go on—and Marx did. He was incensed by the power of religion to domesticate lively human thought and stifle the spirit of resentment and rebellion against the status quo. Religion, he believed, had to be destroyed and eradicated, no matter how natural it was to the human spirit, because it prevented humankind from taking its destiny into its own hands. It made strong and intelligent men and women content with the fates they were in no way obliged to endure. They did not have to work fourteen hours a day in "dark, satanic mills" (as Blake would call them) and die at age forty of malnutrition and spiritual listlessness. They did not have to raise up sons to become cannon fodder for the armies of the powerful. No law of nature prescribed ignorance for the many and learning only for a few. None of this was inevitable, everything could be changed now, and here!

But the change—the revolution—could only occur when men and women stopped believing in their hearts that the gods had set them in their classes and stations just as surely as they had set the stars in the heavens. Humanity could only achieve its real potential if it sent the gods packing! (It may occur to the reader that the climate in which Marx came to such radical conclusions was the same climate that encouraged most of the immigrants to these shores of ours to pack up their own bags and see whether they could not get a second chance at life in this New World. The modern vision has this common ground, after all, whether it is entertained in communistic or in more individualistic (free-enterprise) terms. It is not really surprising, then, that for all their rhetoric and their official enmity, the Russians and the Americans often look to the rest of the world like ideological first cousins).

Letting the Critique Sink In

Is religion an opiate, a repressive drug, the little bit of sugar that helps the medicine go down? Is the Christian religion just a particular brand of that placebo—perhaps an especially effective and

sophisticated form, suitable to the psychic needs of the
"advanced" people of Western civilization? Is prayer, therefore,
undertaken in the name of the One who resigned himself to a cross,
simply a ritual means for imbibing the opiate?

Whatever Christians may think of Karl Marx's general pro-
gram (and fortunately the church seems broad enough to include a
whole spectrum of opinion on that subject), no Christian, whatever
his or her theology, ecclesiology, or politics, can afford to ignore
Marx's critique of religion. Of course, that critique predates Karl
Marx. The prophets and reformers already, in their way, knew a
good deal about the repressive functioning of religion—read again
the myth of the tower of Babel.

Since the alternative religion that Marx helped launch in the
modern world, explicit religion of every variety is obliged to live
with Marx's question. Is what we are doing in this church, congregation, Sunday school, prayer meeting, or seminary part of the
repressive mechanics of a culture that wants to avoid certain things,
criticisms, and types of awareness? Are we, who are teachers and
ministers and elders in our religious communities, helping to prepare young people and others to live in society as uncritical, docile,
"happy" folk, who can always be counted on to say that it's all for
the best? Is it for the best that fewer and fewer people in the advanced
technological society are able to find meaningful work and do not
have the means of leisure? That increasing numbers of the young go
all the way in the act of repression and turn themselves off with
drugs, alcohol, sex, and mindless entertainment, overt religion having become ineffectual for many of them? That the greatest human
resourcefulness and energy is devoted to controlling nature and preparing to kill other human beings? Are we Christians part of a net-
work of agencies and influences that is equipping our own and future
generations of women actually to enjoy housework and think that
little girls were made for washing up pots and pans and crocheting
little things to dress up the home? Is the spirituality in which we are
steeped, and which we hope to inculcate, such that it is almost con-
stitutionally afraid of ever saying no?

What are we doing when we pray, "Father in heaven, teach us to accept the trials and tribulations of this earthly life, bowing to thy holy will, after the example of thy blessed Son our Lord, and in the knowledge that our reward in the life to come will more than compensate for these present sufferings. . . ."? So many of the prayers of the church—not only its historic collects, but the more informal contemporary prayers as well—still have this sort of flavor.

There are, of course, times and places where precisely something like that has to be prayed. But what happens to a people—perhaps to a whole civilization—when something like this is the norm? Prayer is pedagogy of a very effective kind, sometimes to the point of being sheer conditioning. What is communicated about the nature of things when Sunday after Sunday, and at home in private devotions, Christians are placed under the influence of such intensive and intimate pedagogy?

What seems to be conveyed about reality in much of our praying, reduced to crass principles, is the following:

1. The world is a painful place, for which we should nevertheless be unqualifiedly grateful (prayers of thanksgiving), and for whose welfare we should of course pray (prayers of intercession), but of which we should not expect too much.

2. What happens is meant to happen—after all, God is in charge (prayers of adoration). We should resign ourselves to our lot, no matter whether it is pleasant or woeful (prayers of assent).

3. Jesus was a gentle and obedient man, and he is our model for such resignation.

4. The "real thing" only happens when we are dead. Therefore, our best course of action now is to adjust ourselves to the present and wait in hope for the reward that will be given to those who endure this worldly testing ground.

This sounds rather close to the thing that Marx could not abide about religion. Most middle-class North American churchgoers can't abide it either; but instead of saying so straightforwardly they practice a little theological sleight-of-hand, designed to give them a better conscience about the fact that what they were taught to wait for in heaven has quite delightfully already begun to show up in their backyards along with patios and hot tubs! They perform an exercise, so to speak, in realized eschatology.

But neither the more classical/orthodox spirituality that is prepared to wait for heaven's compensations, nor the bourgeois/revisionist spirituality that is glad to find heaven anticipated in its living room—neither is able or willing to take the step that Marx insisted had to be taken to bring about change. The old-time religion contents itself with spiritual change, personal conversion and repentance (which in practice means an even more willing acceptance of the social and economic status quo), and the new-time religion of the affluent already has all the change it wants.

A Critique of the Critique

Of course, Karl Marx was not right about everything. He was a nineteenth-century man who, just like other eighteenth- and nineteenth-century visionaries too soon discarded the old, dark, medieval knowledge that some things cannot be changed—that there is a destiny over against which we must work out our freedom, and that human greatness and courage are more mysterious than the heroics of the revolutionaries. Marx was typically nineteenth century in his minimization of what I have been in the habit of calling the experience of negation.[18] The threatening, negating darkness at the edge of our consciousness can never be wholly banished—not by us, anyway. Perhaps in the last analysis it even serves an indispensable and positive purpose. In any case, part of what faith in Jesus Christ means, perhaps the deepest part, is the courage to live with the darkness, the vision to see the light that only shines in that darkness (see John 1:5).

Marx was perfectly right when he insisted that the point is not just to understand the world but to change it.[19] Jesus, who prayed that his disciples would be enabled to live in the world obediently in spite of "the evil one," would have agreed with that insistence—as far as it went.

But it didn't go far enough. In its enthusiasm for the positive, for action, for revolution and change, it forgot the presence and power of "the evil one." It also forgot the courage that is born of contemplation and the hope that springs from visions that can never be wholly realized. For transformation can and often must mean gaining a new perspective on what is there, not just exchanging what is there for something reputedly new and different.

Reinhold Niebuhr understood Marx's strength in this matter; but he also knew the strength of the prophetic traditions of Israel and the church from which Marx drew, in part, his inspiration. So when Niebuhr prayed for the courage to change things he also prayed for the serenity to accept what could not be changed—and, what is most important, for the wisdom to discern the difference between them.[20]

Chapter 2

Strategic Disengagement

And in the morning, a great while before day, he rose and went out to a lonely place, and there he prayed. And Simon and those who were with him pursued him, and they found him and said to him, "Every one is searching for you." And he said to them, "Let us go on to the next towns, that I may preach there also; for that is why I came out" (Mark 1:35-38).

Putting Wisdom in Its Place

"Grant us the courage to change what can be changed, the serenity to accept what cannot be changed, and the wisdom to distinguish between them."[21]

Wisdom is not the greatest good for which we as Christians are asked to pray. It was the tradition of Athens, not of Jerusalem, which counseled human beings to seek wisdom above all else. Biblical faith calls its adherents to seek first God's kingdom and the righteousness that comes from God (Matthew 6:32-33, paraphrased); for in the minds of those who over the centuries gave expression to Jerusalem's peculiar faith, we are not saved by knowledge but by repentance, grace, and love. Those of us who live in communities of learning know very well that wisdom is no guarantee of these latter things.

The early church, and in a way the church throughout the ages, had to struggle with the temptation to give wisdom priority over love. Gnosticism, which announced that salvation was through the impartation and appropriation of knowledge (*gnosis*) was officially rejected, finally, in the struggles of the first centuries when Christians attempted to define their faith more precisely over against its aberrations. But something as powerful as the idea that those who are the chosen are the ones who have attained the highest degree of wisdom is not easily laid to rest, and many forms of the church—particularly among us Protestants—have been plagued by the insinuating thought (which Christian intellectuals have done little to discourage) that the real Christians are the theologians, ministers, and professionally trained laypersons who know the most.

Over against all such unwarranted elevation of learning, it must always be said that knowledge and wisdom are secondary matters indeed for our faith tradition. When Paul lists the three primary virtues of Christian belief in 1 Corinthians 13 (faith, hope, and love), wisdom isn't even mentioned. In fact, it is rather summarily put in its place, along with good works and religious zeal, in the process of his argument in that text: "And if I . . . understand all mysteries and all knowledge . . . but have not love, I am nothing" (13:2). For knowledge, like prophecy, like tongues, will pass away, whereas "love never ends . . ." (13:8).

We Impart Wisdom

This relegation of wisdom to a status lower than love, faith, and hope ought not to tempt anyone to conclude that for the biblical tradition wisdom is purely optional or perhaps even a detriment. From the beginning, just as there have been believers who exaggerated the place of knowledge, there have been Christians who have underestimated the importance of wisdom in the life of faith. They have taken the Christian critique of knowledge to mean that they could indulge to the full their natural inclination to mental sloth, or their resentment of all who possess learning. The two extremes have often lived side by side, as extremes are wont to do. An over-emphasis on the need for intellectual comprehension begets a reaction in the form of the sort of pietism that looks upon learning as a cover-up for the lack of belief, and prides itself on its "simple faith."[22]

This is a matter almost uncomfortably close to our present subject, because very often those who make most of the life of prayer in the churches are persons who for one reason or another depreciate serious Christian scholarship and the pursuit of understanding. They can be heard, on occasion, telling one another and all within hearing distance that their simple faith and the equally simple prayer to which it gives spontaneous rise are far more pleasing to God than all the learning of scholars, theologians, and degree-ladened clergy. In this way, prayer becomes a sort of alternative to thought, and, in the bargain, a very self-righteous weapon against all who have devoted their lives to intellectual reflection. In a book of this kind, we can hardly afford to overlook the unfortunate sense in which prayer so often serves the questionable motives of Christian anti-intellectualism. This concern will be more systematically treated in the second part of our study.

For the present, we need only to notice that while wisdom is certainly not the most important ingredient in the Christian life, it is nevertheless a quality that Christians who are serious about their faith will strive for. The same Paul who castigates the (reputedly) "wise" ones for their failure to "know God" through wisdom (1 Corinthians 1:21), goes on to acknowledge the indispensable place of wisdom in the community of belief (2:6). Paul is not talking about "the wisdom of this age," which has too high an opinion of itself to recognize truth when it meets it face to face, and indeed crucifies the truth; but the wisdom of the cross. Because for Paul what God has done in Jesus Christ is not nonsense, despite the fact that the world receives it as such—as plain foolishness. There is a "logic of the cross," according to Reinhold Niebuhr,[23] and Paul's whole vocation, like that of countless Christian thinkers since, is a courageous attempt to articulate that "secret and hidden wisdom of God . . . decreed before the ages for our glorification" (2:7).

Discernment and Discipleship

Wisdom (*sophia*), like every other profound concept of biblical religion—like faith, hope, and love—defies definition in a small book or even in a very large one. But our purposes here make it necessary for us to delve at least a little way into this profundity. We are to think about wisdom as it relates to prayer. Without exhausting even that one dimension of the nature of wisdom as it is conceived in the tradition of Jerusalem, we may nevertheless observe a certain logic also in this relation.

The clue to the connection between wisdom and prayer is implied in Niebuhr's by-now-famous little prayer. Wisdom, he infers, has to do with being able to distinguish between things, to make decisions, to perceive differences, to judge between subtle alternatives of change and acceptance.

Another biblical word—"discernment"—can help us to expand our understanding of what is meant. "It is my prayer," writes the author of Philippians, "that your love may abound more and more with knowledge and all discernment" (1:9). The Greek word used here is *aisthēsis*; the Latin, from which our English word derives directly, is from the same root as the words "disciple" and "discipline"—*discere,* meaning "to learn." The implication is clear: discipleship involves the acquisition of a discerning attitude. It is, I suspect, the same sort of thing that Jesus had in mind when he uttered the rather enigmatic though intriguing proverb that his disciples would have to be "wise as serpents and innocent as doves" (Matthew 10:16), or that the writer of Second Timothy intended when he spoke of "rightly handling [the KJV, more graphically, translates "rightly *dividing*"] the word of "truth" (2:15). Such discernment, or perception, or sensitivity to distinctions, is not the end of the matter (again we must warn ourselves not to make wisdom too exalted). The end of the matter is love: ". . . that your *love* abound more and more" (Philippians 1:9). We are to seek wisdom in order to be enabled to love more appropriately—and obediently. Niebuhr's concise prayer makes essentially the same point. Love is always about serving others; and if we pray for the courage to change, the serenity to accept, and the wisdom to make fine distinctions, it is not for the sake of enhancing our own worth, but in order that our love, our service of the beloved, may be more effective.

Behind this exhortation to discernment is the Bible's frank recognition of the difficulty of living as Christ's disciples in a world of "ambiguities" (to employ again the language of Reinhold Niebuhr). "Look carefully then how you walk," exclaims Paul to the Ephesian Christians "not as unwise men but as wise, making the most of the time, because the days are evil. Therefore do not be foolish, but understand what the will of the Lord is" (Ephesians 5:15-17). He goes on to warn the congregation in that place about the dangers of drunkenness and debauchery and internal dissension in the *koinonia* and modern, moralistically-inclined church-folk can easily mistake all this for a biblical warranty for their own brand of moralism. It is in fact, however, much more serious than that.

It has to do with wisdom—with the need, that is to say, for a clear-headed and penetrating vigilance on the part of those who have been chosen to follow the Christ on his journey into the interior. As we can detect in many other places in the Scriptures (especially, I think, in the wisdom literature of the Old Testament and the Epistles of the New Testament), there is in this literature a great realism about the complications of such a journey. It is not an easy matter to find the right path, to do the right thing for the right reason. It is not easy in the first place even to know what is right. For one thing, we ourselves are only beginners—"on the way" (*in via*). Our personal lives and our life together as the fellowship are plagued by internal confusions. How often throughout these twenty-odd centuries have good Christian intentions been ruined by glandular and other urges, by mixed-up relations within the congregation, by petty jealousies and insidious talk! Besides, this inner confusion is compounded by the great cosmic confusion (as seen in 1 John 5:19) that was as conspicuous in that first century as it is in our own time. "The days are evil" (Ephesians 5:16).

In such days it is, to be sure, love that must abound. For personal and societal chaos creates more victims of human unlove than are found in times of relative social and moral stability. But love as such—love as the will to befriend and cherish and steward one's neighbors and one's world, love as intention and emotion, love as engagement—is not enough. Much shallow thought and indecisive activity claims love as its motive and its means. The world—perhaps especially the world influenced by the rhetoric of Christian love—is full of inept and misguided lovers whose compassion and good will are lost because they have not been honed by discernment. We are not called by Jesus Christ to a life of romantic loving-kindness. We are instead called to a vocation of sober care, to a love that can cut through the social and moral confusion. Walk carefully around the hidden deceptions and wrong turnings that bedevil the way of discipleship, and avoid the foolishness that often passes for cleverness in these evil days. "Be wise!" exhorts the Apostle to the Ephesians, echoing the wisdom traditions of Israel, which also tried to offer guidance to a witnessing community in a diaspora situation. Be wise! Be discerning! As disciples of the Christ, your life should count for something, and not just crown the chaos and superficiality of the age with stained-glass sentimentality.

Perspective

The wisdom of faithful discipleship means discernment, the capacity to distinguish, to see nuances, and to make keen judgments. But such a capacity is not given to anyone as a matter of course, and it cannot be learned simply, as one learns a mathematics table or the Ten Commandments. Such discernment requires time, patience, and the steady contemplation of the gospel. It requires a vantage point from which to assess what is happening. Where is the journey taking us? It requires perspective to understand.

Each of us knows how vital it is to his or her own life to keep gaining perspective on what is occurring around and within one. Without what we have come to call an overview, without at least some minimal organization of our priorities around certain fairly clear-cut values, we are pushed about from one moment to the next, one relationship to another, one momentary preoccupation to some other that temporarily seems more vital. In the age of mass communications and the knowledge explosion, it is very hard to sustain perspective. Like the biblical people who are described as being "carried about by every wind of doctrine" (Ephesians 4:14), we feel ourselves vacillating with every news broadcast, every new bestseller, every latest interpretation of events. We are at the mercy of powerful image makers and formulators of public opinion. Wisdom, for us as for the Ephesian congregation, would surely have to mean an ongoing quest for the kind of perspective that could lift us out of dependency relationships—dependence upon the media, upon government-controlled channels of information, upon the explanations of experts and authorities who are seldom without their own vested interests in the public meaning of events.

Perspective implies a sense of direction. We may be on the way, but where are we going? The Greeks, truly experts where the quest for wisdom is concerned, had an instructive term in this connection: *telos*. It means "end" or "goal" or "inner aim," for the goal is that which, from within, directs our progress and our growth. The telos of an acorn is to become an oak tree. The potentiality for the great, enduring tree is already there in the tiny acorn.

Paul tells the Ephesians that Christians, too, have a telos. They are in the process of becoming mature human beings—humanity defined by the truly human (*vere homo*) person, Jesus the Christ. Our telos is to attain "to the measure of the stature of the fulness of Christ" (Ephesians 4:13). If we keep our faith fixed upon this goal, this human person, we shall not be "tossed to and fro and carried about by every wind of doctrine" (Ephesians 4:14). This end of our journey as people of the way (*communio viatorum*) is not only the final stage, the longed-for attainment of the "prize" at the end of "the race" (see 1 Corinthians 9:24). It is also a vision and vantage point from which we may here and now derive perspective and a sense of direction. To be sure, we cannot claim the untrammelled sight of those who have arrived at their destination ("we see in a mirror dimly"—1 Corinthians 13:12). Our perspective is that of faith and of hope, not of sight (Hebrews 11:1; Romans 8:24-25). Yet this hope is sufficient; the perspective that it offers "does not disappoint us" (Romans 5:5). For the telos of our pilgrimage is already present to us, around us, within us—even our "present sufferings" confirm it! (see Romans 8:18). For, far from depending upon our own capacity for the journey, our determination, our optimism, the sense of direction and meaning that we require is a gift of God's love that has been "poured into our hearts through the Holy Spirit . . ." (Romans 5:5).

Maintaining Perspective in a Non-Teleological Universe

Wisdom implies discernment, discernment requires perspective, perspective is derived from a sense of direction, and that sense is the gift of the Spirit.

All the same, it is easy to lose one's way!

When reading the Pauline and other expressions of the spiritual wisdom that belongs to Christian discipleship, Christians today are apt to become discouraged. For the loss of a sense of purpose is almost palpable in contemporary society, and Christians are by no means immune to the loss. People in stable, well-ordered civilizations, such as the Christian Middle Ages are reputed to have been, are often described as living in a teleological universe—a world shot through and through with meaning. They do not have to wake up every morning and ask themselves, full of *angst*, what their purpose might be—suspecting that absolutely no purpose can be found.

By comparison, ours is decidedly not a teleological universe. How can one sustain a sense of purpose in a world that even scientists say is moving closer to doomsday? That is hardly a telos calculated to inspire enthusiasm for the journey! What would it take to feel that the world is being directed by some inner aim in the age of future shock? For some of our fellow Christians, whom we met briefly in the Introduction, it seems to require abandoning hope for this world altogether. They can keep hold of a sense of purpose for themselves, perhaps, but only by insulating themselves from the rest of society, turning their churches quite literally into sanctuaries, and leaving history to heaven. Or to hell.

But can the "love poured into our hearts through the Holy Spirit," the love that should abound, so soon dispense with the world? Is the rest of creation to be abandoned by this spontaneous and unmotivated love that none of us deserve?

Paul, our teacher of wisdom, thinks otherwise. "For the creation waits with eager longing for the revealing of the sons of God; for the creation was subjected to futility, not of its own will but by the will of him who subjected it *in hope; because the creation itself will be set free from its bondage to decay and obtain the glorious liberty of the children of God*" (Romans 8:19-21, emphasis mine).

Amen! Many of us, Christians and non-Christians alike, want to believe that. Yet in spite of our fervent hope for the redemption of "groaning" creation (see Romans 8:22), we are fearfully tempted to doubt the prospect. What is worse, this doubt assails those who are most committed to the earth and its healing! For them, when they are persons of faith, religion is no "opiate." It is more nearly a source of pain. For it goads them into hope, into planning, into tending, into work for the future—and there seems so little concrete evidence that such vision is justified or reasonable. How can one maintain Paul's perspective of creation set free from bondage to decay in a nonteleological universe?

The Plight of Those Who Love
Before we respond to this key question, we shall have to deepen it

because it really is more complex than it appears. It is not just that our contemporary, technology-driven society, lacking a teleological sense, infects even believers with doubt concerning the human and worldly prospect. The danger of losing perspective belongs to the life of discipleship as such. It was as much a danger for Paul's Ephesians as it is for us. The source of the danger, paradoxically, is the very love which, as those who are the recipients of love, we are commanded and enabled to show forth in all that we do.

This is a paradox. But paradoxes are neither contradictions nor nonsense. They contain some rudimentary, if strange and sometimes unsettling, logic. It is not ridiculous if we say that love is in a profound and mysterious way the source of the danger that disciples of the Christ may lose their powers of discernment, their perspective. For to love is to be thoroughly involved in the life of what (or whom) is loved. To love is not to hold back, not to reserve some part of oneself, not to calculate the cost to one's own person. "Love does not insist on its own way; it is not irritable or resentful; it does not rejoice at wrong, but rejoices in the right. Love bears all things, believes all things, hopes all things, endures all things (1 Corinthians 13:5-7). Love is being-with and being-for the other, to the point of risking the loss of self. It is the most intensive form of communion—of engagement.

How does one sustain a sense of perspective when one is so intensely engaged? The plight of those who love is that their very closeness to the object of their deepest concern frequently robs them of perspective. Thus it is not really surprising that it is often those who are most concerned for the future of the earth who are most susceptible to doubt and despair. Just because they are not able to be dispassionate, as the hopeless are dispassionate, they are constantly in danger of losing their sense of direction.

It was always so. The plight of love, which is perennial, is of course aggravated by social conditions of the sort through which we are now passing—the chaotic churning of history, the shaking of the foundations. However, the early church and Christians throughout the ages who have cared about this groaning creation have always known this plight. Jesus himself knew it more intensely than any of us, for his love was complete.

The Place of Wisdom in the Life of Prayer

That is why Jesus prayed and sought out God in solitude, early in the morning, away from the others, away from the world itself. Jesus, too, needed to regain perspective.

Prayer is that mode of reflection, that communication with transcendence, through which the disciples of Jesus, like their Lord himself, seek to gain and regain just this perspective and this teleological sense that they need if they are to be a community of discerning love. Wisdom in the service of love is the human intellect at prayer.

Such reflection requires a certain distancing of oneself from the world, from the immediate, from the rush and tumble of existence. There can be no doubt that this distancing of the disciple community is an integral part of the Bible's conception of the nature and vocation of God's covenant people in both biblical testaments. Not only did Jesus himself frequently seek solitude as the context of prayer, but his life with the original Twelve was clearly a mixture of engagement and disengagement *vis à vis* the larger human community. The Markan account of what happened upon the return of the disciples from their first mission abroad is typical of this dialectic of involvement and detachment.

> The apostles returned to Jesus, and told him all that they had done and taught. And he said to them, "Come away by yourselves to a lonely place, and rest a while." For many were coming and going and they had no leisure even to eat (Mark 6:30-31).

The New Testament's understanding of prayer is very much informed by the principle of disengagement, of withdrawal. Jesus advises his hearers when praying to " . . . go into your room and shut the door and pray to your Father who is in secret . . . " (Matthew 6:6). Against the ostentation and boastful piety of "the hypocrites" (6:5), he counsels his disciples to practice prayer quietly

and modestly. It is not a public thing. There is something ludi-
crous, given such biblical counsel, about praying before a television audience of millions! But the fundamental reason for the
privacy and quietness of prayer in Jesus' teaching is not just his
abhorrence of ostentation. It is, more positively considered, his
awareness of the fact that prayer is intended to speak to our need to
be free of all outside interference, all consciousness of being
observed, all preoccupation with appearances. In prayer, the
Christian and the Christian community distance themselves from
their world. They are not there to impress anybody, least of all
God. They pray because they need to pray. They have to acquire or
reacquire the sense of perspective, direction, and purpose that is
always in danger of slipping away into the background, upstaged by
the immediacy of the mission. Their love and eagerness to be under
way must be seasoned with wisdom.

It is imperative for Christians today to learn this habit of strategic disengagement. It is particularly necessary for those among us
who are in some real sense the most engaged disciples of the Christ
in these evil days. Just because the evil is so rampant, one feels
committed to an unresting vigilance. The principalities and powers
that are destroying God's good but groaning creation do not
observe the sabbath. Hence, many of the most sensitive contemporary Christians feel that they, too, cannot afford the luxury of contemplation.

But without such contemplation we easily become contribu-
tors to the very confusion that we hope to arrest. Our activities may
be entirely sincere, motivated by unusual love of the world and all
its creatures. But if we ourselves have lost our way, even our good
concerns and deeds are apt to add to the evil that they are meant to
deter. The world—the church, too—is well endowed with high-
intentioned activists who, because they are not clear about the
right questions, unwittingly become part of the world's wrong
answers. Nothing is more necessary in the last fifth of the twentieth
century than a faith that has seasoned love with real discernment—
that is able to distinguish, in the light of its prayerful contemplation

of the will of the Lord, what ought to be changed and what may be serenely accepted. I can only consider it deplorable when I hear Christians dismissing others (usually other Christians) as "mere activists." In a world where so many are passive, or act only for their own security and aggrandizement, any activity directed towards the public realm should be admired even when it is ineffectual or frenzied. Yet Christian activism (or *praxis*, or better "obedience") requires a prayerful distancing of ourselves from the world. No chastisement on the part of activists, who are prone to find any sort of distancing a kind of betrayal, should deter the Christian community from this strategic disengagement, the *conditio sine qua non* of discerning love.

We have to be entirely clear when we say that it is for engagement that we disengage. We go away to the quiet place in order to come still closer to the world. It is for proximity that we seek to regain perspective. It is for a purposive being in the world that, in prayer, we reclaim our identity with an eternity that is not of the world. It is for understanding the difference that we seek spiritual discernment. It is for love of the world that we strive for a wisdom that is hidden from the world.

Therefore, let us go on.

Chapter 3

Consecrated Worldliness

For everything created by God is good, and nothing is to be rejected if it is received with thanksgiving; for then it is consecrated by the word of God and prayer (1 Timothy 4:4-5).

Becoming Human

The confronting question of our study on the purpose of prayer is whether prayer is a way of extricating oneself from the world or of achieving greater proximity to it. Is prayer an escape hatch or a doorway to reality? When we pray, are we attempting to "get away from it all" or to stay with it?

In the first chapter, we reminded ourselves that one of the most effective modern critics of religion rejected the religious impulse because he saw it as an irresponsible escapism, robbing human society of the will to assume a more direct role in the destiny of the race. In the second chapter, we affirmed that prayer does involve a necessary element of disengagement, a distancing of ourselves from the world. The purpose of this detachment, however, is by no means escapist; rather, it is to enable us to achieve new levels of attachment and commitment to the world's life through the acquisition of a wisdom that can season our love. If prayer is a matter of coming apart and being separate, it is this as a means and not as an end. The goal of prayer is for human beings to become more truly human, that we might make good our identity as creatures of this world.

Such a conception of the nature and purpose of prayer may seem offensive to some who read this book. I have no wish to offend, and certainly no interest in maintaining positions for their shock value. I am entirely in earnest about the definition of prayer implied in the heading of this chapter and this subsection—that prayer means becoming truly worldly. Its purpose is not to remove us from the world or remove the world from us. Its purpose is to put us into the world in a more intentional, unreserved way, and to consecrate what is best of the world that is in us.

World-wariness

Let us begin to elaborate by considering the more negative side of the matter. If we ask why certain conventional forms of Christian piety find a statement like "prayer is our means of becoming more truly worldly" to be shocking or heretical, the answer is not far away or difficult to grasp. It is grounded in the habit of setting God and this world over against each other, as mutually exclusive alternatives for human concern, loyalty, and love. This habit may be as old as humanity itself, and, as I shall try to show presently, it is strangely related to what the biblical tradition calls "sin." But it was given a special boost in the early church by the encounter of Christianity, whose original expression was in the Hebraic mode, with forms of religious and philosophic thought within the so-called Hellenistic milieu that were deeply suspicious of the material universe.

All through the tradition of Athens, in its high philosophical expression as well as its more popular forms, there runs a profound wariness with respect to this world, and especially its physical or material reality. Plato called the human body *sōma sēma*—the "body tomb." Our soul (*psychē*) is imprisoned in our body. Our intellects, which represent the highest aspect of our spiritual being, are hampered continuously by the passions which emanate from our flesh (*sarx*). We are constantly dragged down by emotions and attachments to material and sensory things. Thus we are prevented from attaining the perfection to which our spirits and minds are heir.

In popular religion, this abhorrence of matter and the body gave rise to cults and rituals and practices which had, as their object, the freeing of the soul from its bondage to cloying, degrading material embodiment. If what is wrong with human beings is their finitude, their enfleshment, then the correction for it has to be some method of liberation from matter and its allurements and limitations. In this life there must begin a detachment from matter—something that can undoubtedly only be brought to completion after death, when the soul has been freed from the body altogether. Through a strict asceticism, through rituals of sacrificial or liturgical identification with dying and rising gods, through a stringent and concentrated cultivation of the mind to accompany the disciplining and spartan pommelling of the body (see 1 Corinthians 9:27), one might approximate already on earth that affinity with the immortal that was the soul's true origin and destiny.

Early Christians were by no means insensitive to the appeal of such a view of existence. How could they be? When Christianity moved out beyond the boundaries of Judaism and the synagogues of the ancient Jewish Diaspora; when it became a mission to the Gentiles, this was the spiritual climate that it encountered everywhere. Indeed, it met this spirituality within Judaism, for Judaism itself had been influenced by the Hellenistic world. Thus, with many important figures of the early Christian centuries (including Origen, Tertullian, and Augustine), it is possible to detect distinct echoes of this world-wariness.

Not untypical of the period is the practice of dividing the human race into three categories. The highest quality of personhood (the so-called *pneumatikoi* = the"spiritual" people) were those who had achieved the most impressive transcendence of matter. The lowest (the *sarkikoi* = the "fleshy" or "earthy" people) were those who were obviously at the mercy of the passions. The *psychikoi*—those "in between on the misty flats," might go either one way or the other, depending upon influences brought to bear upon them.[24]

The Good Earth

This deep suspicion and fear of materiality, concentrating of course upon the flesh and the so-called sins and weaknesses thereof, is not compatible with the Hebraic milieu in which Christianity first took root. I do not mean that Jewish faith simply celebrated the flesh in a mindless, "Age-of-Aquarius" sort of way. That is a modern distortion of biblical faith. It achieved a certain prominence in the 1960s, which produced, among other absurdities, images of a laughing young Jesus who had more in common with Dionysius or Bacchus than with the God of Abraham, Isaac, and Jacob. The formulators of Israel's traditions of law, prophecy, and wisdom were not so naive about the dangers of the world, the flesh, and the devil. No one can meditate seriously on the Decalogue, not to mention the many juristic elaborations of the Deuteronomist or the proverbs and spiritual reflections of the wisdom writers, and come away thinking that Judaism was unambiguously satisfied with the way things are. The Old Testament knows just as well as any Neoplatonist or puritan moralist that there are terrifying consequences for all human beings who simply give in to their so-called animal instincts, or even try to do so. The ancient Hebraic authors are perfectly well aware of the fact that there is pain in the world, some of it inherent in the very structures of material embodiment, some of it even necessary pain.[25] They do not assume that the world is perfect according to some utopian conception of perfection.

But they do assume that the world is good. The first account of creation, chronologically later than the account of Genesis chapter

2 but perhaps for this very reason theologically and canonically first, sets the tone for the whole story: "And God saw everything that he had made, and behold, it was very good" (Genesis 1:31). This is where the real difference between the spirituality that tended to dominate in the tradition of Athens and that of Jerusalem lies. For Israel, creation is good. The earth is good, because it is God's own work. It is God's project, and even if it is a fallen creation, it is still God's earth. And God's whole object, to quote contemporary Jewish scholar Emil Fackenheim, is creation's mending.[26]

Hence, in the Judaic approach, there can be no ultimate opposition between creation and Creator. There can be no question of choosing between loyalty to the one and not the other. There can be no love of God that is hatred of the world. There can be no turning towards God that is turning away from God's world. Like the old American proverb, "Love me, love my dog," the God of Israel insists, "Love me, love my world."

Christian Worldlessness

But what about the New Testament? Did John and Paul and the others overtly or covertly reject this basic Jewish orientation? Were they perhaps converted to a more Athenian form of spirituality, one that looked for salvation in the castigation and dethronement of the flesh, the liberation of the soul from the body, and the rejection of this evil and fallen world in favor of a transubstantial or supramundane otherworld?

One has to admit that the question is not easily answered. Much of the language of the Gospel of John, some of the Epistles, and the Revelation sounds as though these writers had resolved the tensions of body and spirit—of which the prophets, lawgivers, and wisdom writers of Israel were well aware—by coming over to the side of the spiritualizers. Indeed, a text like James 4:4, which states, "Do you not know that friendship with the world is enmity with God? Therefore whoever wishes to be a friend of the world makes himself an enemy of God" appears to condone the most world-negating sentiments of all, whose cry is some variation on the theme, "Stop the world, I want to get off!"

So entrenched is the supposition that Christianity at its truest and most spiritual is unworldly or anti-worldly that some of the most sensitive and devout persons of our epoch have been deeply affected by it. This applies both to some who were and remained Christians despite Christianity's reputation for unworldliness and to others who rejected Christian belief precisely on that account. One of the former was Pierre Teilhard de Chardin. Teilhard could not renounce his "delight" in "this luminous world" [27] despite his suspicion, nurtured by centuries of saintly world-renunciation, that that was what the traditions of the faith as well as its present-day guardians expected of him. In his work as theologian and scientist, he set for himself the task of communicating "the reconciliation of God and the world." Of his 1916 monograph, *Cosmic Life,* he wrote:

> I offer it to those who are chary of accepting Christ, because they suspect him of wishing to besmirch the fair face of the earth to which their love is irrevocably pledged; and I offer it to those, too, who, in order to love Christ, force themselves to turn their backs on what fills their souls to overflowing; and to those, finally, who have been unable to bring together as one the God of their faith and the God of their most ennobling labors, and who grow weary and impatient of a life that is dissipated in misdirected effort. [28]

Among those who, while respecting aspects of Christian belief, had to turn away in sorrow, none is more instructive than the great Jewish humanist sage, Hannah Arendt. Her biographer, Elisabeth Young-Bruehl, writes of Arendt's "completely non-Christian understanding of the common world." She assesses Arendt's position in that way because Arendt's whole life-work was offered "for love of the world" (the subtitle of Young-Bruehl's biography). From Augustine, on whom she did her doctoral dissertation (under Karl Jaspers), Arendt learned that "worldlessness" is "the main Christian principle," and that what replaces love of the world in Christianity is love of the brethren. This "brotherly love" (*caritas*), writes Arendt, "is admirably fit[ted] to carry a group of essentially worldless people through the world . . . provided only that it is understood that the world itself is doomed and that every activity is undertaken with the proviso *quandiu mundus durat* ('as long as the world lasts')." Such a posture serves a religion whose primary concern is the salvation of one's soul; but as soon as one asks about the fate of that earthly context where souls are born and shaped, it is entirely inadequate and perhaps detrimental. For "the common world . . . lasts as long as men care for it and are able to save it." [29]

Is worldlessness of the essence of Christian faith? It has been thought so by both Christians and non-Christians and it has been presented in such a light, even by some of Christianity's most formative interpreters. But is world renunciation what the Christ is all about, what faith is all about, and what prayer is all about? Is worldlessness scriptural?

We can by no means resolve all the issues involved in this question, to which biblical and historical scholarship has given lifetimes of attention over the past century, in a small study on prayer. But we can and must clarify our personal position on the topic. Three observations will be made.

Distinguishing World Rejection and Prophetic Indignation

First, large issues like whether the New Testament is anti- or pro-world should not be settled by quoting isolated texts or even sections of the Scriptures. If you look at the context even of a stark statement like the one from the Epistle of James quoted previously (4:4), you will see at once that the author's concern is not the grand doctrinal enterprise of asking whether the gospel is or is not world-affirming. The issue is more explicit: how should a young congregation, surrounded by worldly temptations, be instructed in the working out of its communal life? Like most other biblical writers, James is highly critical of the values and pursuits of the dominant culture that is the congregation's socioeconomic context. Indeed, any religious or secular system of meaning that wants to change the world is going to be steeped in passionate denunciations of society or sorrowful expressions of what is wrong with the world. That is eminently true of Karl Marx, Hannah Arendt, and present-day liberation theology.

But as Marx, Arendt, and the liberationists all demonstrate, even intensely negative assessments of what is going on in the world do not, necessarily, betoken an attitude that says, "Let us be done with this damned, doomed thing! Let us save our own skins!" In fact, most of the prophetic denunciations of the world that are found either in the Bible or in great theology throughout the ages are really not denunciations of the world as such but of what human beings have made of the world. They are inspired by prophetic indignation over the spoilage by thoughtless or evil persons and agencies of what is in essence a very good thing. It is their sense of the essential goodness of the world that fires their denunciation of what the world has become.

What We Hear and What Is There

Second, what we hear in the Bible is very often determined not by what is actually there, but by what we have come to expect to find there. Our expectations are fed by many sources and conventions that may well prove not only to be nonscriptural but also actually contrary to Scripture.

A case in point that is closely connected with the subject of prayer is related to what we were saying earlier about the Greek quest for aligning the soul with its immortal origin and ground. Generations of Christians, even in parishes where the Apostles' Creed, with its, " . . . and I believe in the resurrection of the body . . . " is recited, have supposed in their hearts that Christian dogma teaches the immortality of the soul. Their whole way of handling concepts like the resurrection, life after death, the Last Judgment, and so forth, betrays a spiritual-intellectual ethos that belongs to the tradition of Athens, not of Jerusalem.

Thus, when such persons go to a passage of Scripture like 1 Corinthians 15, where Paul takes on the knotty problem of what the resurrection of Jesus means for our post-historical destiny as Christians, they hear Paul affirming that the soul after death resumes its essential immortality, the risen Lord having given it its long-awaited liberation from the terrestrial body. Whereas in reality Paul's whole struggle in that important but difficult passage of his letter to the Corinthians is to speak precisely about the resurrection of the body. He does not succeed very well, of course. Theology at this point can't succeed and mustn't pretend to succeed. Resurrection is God's possibility—not a commonplace of history or a law of nature. It is a matter of sheer grace. But Paul tries to explain it anyway because he is conscious of so many false theologies hovering around this subject—including, very prominently, that same Greek tendency to resolve the whole issue by denigrating the body and looking upon death as a release from its bondage. For Paul the Jew that kind of resolution simply won't do because it implies that God had no business making bodies to begin with. Or that some other inferior and perhaps malevolent deity had done it as a sort of existential dirty trick. The Hebraic Paul means to uphold the essential goodness and beauty of the body as God's own work. With that in mind he undertakes this prolix and complicated explanation of the resurrection body, the spiritual body. He is not talking about immortality of the soul, but unfortunately a great many Christians expect him to do just that. So that is precisely what they hear in 1 Corinthians 15 and in a good many other places, too. This has the long-range effect of confirming that what is wrong with this world is that it is a poor, material thing for which there is no ultimate cure except its replacement by something better—some heavenly Jerusalem.

"The Word Became Flesh"

Third, and most important: We Christians need to learn how to confront our "religious" temptation to world rejection or ambigu-

ity about creation by contemplating with greater spiritual serious-
ness and intellectual rigor the most central dogma of our faith
tradition: the incarnation. "The Word became flesh and dwelt
among us . . ." (John 1:14).

> Christian devotion and prayer needs to be more humanized, more
> sensitized, less concerned with the inner world in isolation from the
> demands of the poor and hungry, more concerned with the hallowing
> of the world and the transfiguring of the flesh,

writes British theologian Kenneth Leech.[30] The incarnation
means, among many other things, that Hebraic spirituality knows
nothing of an orientation towards God that is not at the same time
an orientation towards God's good earth. In this tradition, God,
too, is turned towards the world. God, too, is anthropocentric and
geocentric. Leech continues:

> We need to develop the facility for turning simultaneously inwards
> to God who is at the centre of our beings, and outwards to the chil-
> dren of God, made in his image and shining in the world. Twenty
> years ago, the late Fr. Geoffrey Curtis observed that "the whole con-
> cept of contemplation is still *in need of being fully incarnationa-
> lized.*" His words abide; the task remains urgent.[31]

The incarnation of the Word of God is not, for Christians, an
incidental or secondary aspect of the gospel—it is the very core of
it. From this center every other facet of Christian belief derives its
fullest meaning. This central event of the story that is told in the
continuity of the testaments confirms God's gracious but resolute
movement towards the creation. God will be Emmanuel, God-
with-us! The God who visits and dwells with us in the flesh could
hardly expect us to become despisers of the flesh.

If God's object were to turn us away from this material world,
with its limitations and temptations, then God chose a very strange
form of exemplification for such pedagogy. If God had really
wanted disembodied spirits as covenant partners then, in addition
to refraining from making bodies in the first place, God would

certainly have proceeded directly to Pentecost and thus eliminated all that even more unseemly work of the conception, birth, life, suffering, death, and resurrection of the Word! Any Christian who pursues redemption as a flight from the world is ill-advised to seek his or her model in the crucified One. Such a Christian had better go directly to the upper room and have as little as possible to do with the cowstall at Bethlehem and the cross on Golgotha. Indeed, the history of Christian spirituality amply demonstrates that more than a few have understood this intuitively. If the Holy Spirit can be sufficiently disengaged from the second Person of the Trinity, then the Spirit makes an excellent theistic principle on the basis on which to construct a spiritualized gospel whose function is to translate flesh-and-blood human beings into disembodied souls.

But precisely that is why the second-century church rejected Montanism,[32] and why in the sixth century the Western church added the so-called *filioque* clause to the Nicene Creed's article concerning the Spirit,[33] and why in the twentieth century numerous spiritualistic sects and charismatics have been the subject of criticism by historical and critical theology. The gospel of Jesus Christ is not concerned with turning people into lovely spirits who long for union with the great Spirit, but with turning persons who are trying to escape form their creaturehood into beings who are content to be God's creatures. These creatures are to inhabit and steward the earth, and live in willed solidarity with all of God's other creatures.

Learning to Affirm Our Creaturehood

We have seen something of why there is a peculiarly religious temptation, operative at some level in all of us, to be otherworldly and so to reject the idea that prayer has to do with becoming worldly. Now let us try to say why Christians should not be tempted to otherworldliness, and should find it both liberating and impeccably Christian to think of spirituality in worldly terms.

It comes down to sin again, of course. What exactly is sin, anyway? For the most part we have been encouraged by religious convention to think of sin as being too worldly. The most popular conceptions of sin—so popular, indeed, that they have been responsible for the mental and physical ruin of millions of human beings—are those that associate sin with worldliness, especially with the body and its lusts. The very word "lust" excites the mind. Sin and sex are synonyms, for all practical purposes, in the minds of vast numbers of North Americans. The great sinners, some of whom have built their fame and fortune on that fact, are the ones who have indulged their lusts as rampantly as possible. The morally righteous wince over the lurid tales that are told of Hollywood sex symbols and the rich and vulgar. Yet there is always a touch of fascination in the indignation of the righteous. Most of us, in perhaps a deeper-than-religious sense, would like to live it up just like these great sinners. Of course, they lived it up absurdly—and often adolescently—so that they simply burned themselves out in the process.

But what if sin were not living it up? What if mortal sin—the sin against the Lord and Giver of life—were holding back, standing nervously at the edge of life and shivering like a scared teenager on a high diving board? What if sin were holding back from expending ourselves, from testing and risking our powers, from getting into the swim?

In his wonderful poem, *A Child's Christmas in Wales,* Dylan Thomas speaks lovingly about the village aunties, who at the Christmas celebrations of the clan "sat on the edges of their chairs, like faded cups and saucers, afraid to break." [34] What if sin were comprised chiefly of that kind of timidity, that strange combination of pride ("Oh, I wouldn't want to be caught doing that!") and sloth ("Oh, I just haven't the mind, the gifts, the energy for that!"), which keeps one from entering into life with a will? What if sin were our refusal to accept our creaturehood with its limitations and its possibilities? What if sin were our constant longing for another kind of world, life, or universe? What if sin were waiting for some ship that might come in, some lottery ticket that may pay off, some prince that might kiss us and turn us into beautiful and desirable creatures, or some savior that might lift us clear out of this vale of tears? What if sin were, in short, our failure or refusal to become what we are: children of the world?

Isn't Genesis chapter 3 all about dissatisfaction with creation, the longing for something else, the wish to be something or someone else—to be gods, perhaps? Isn't that also rather reminiscent of what was going on at the judgment pavement of Pontius Pilate? "I came that they might have *life* . . . abundantly!" (John 10:10, paraphrased) said the one who was being judged there. But they didn't want life. They were afraid of life. They preferred the safe, ordered, predictable existence that they had under Rome—even if it meant their spiritual enslavement and included the violence of Barabbas and the opportunism of Herod. Life came very close to them—and life comes very close to us. But we are afraid, like faded cups and saucers.

Of course, a profound and ancient subject like sin cannot be exhausted of its meaning in a few pages of a theological book. Sin, like the grace by which our sin is met, is an enduring mystery. But if that mystery does not have something quite explicit to do with this frightened but arrogant refusal of human beings to accept and rejoice in their humanity, to receive at God's hands and with thanksgiving their own creatureliness, then I have gravely misunderstood not only sin but the whole tradition of Jerusalem.

Moreover, if sin is backing away from life, then redemption must be "the courage to be" (Tillich). The Good News must be the costly grace through which that courage has been offered us; faith must be our trusting the gift and the Giver; and hope must be looking for a greater unfolding of the possibilities inherent in our creaturehood.

And prayer? Well, in that case, surely prayer would have to mean our daily asking for that courage: "Give us this day our daily bread" (Matthew 6:11). Prayer would have to mean a ceaseless, ongoing dialogue, by means of which we were enabled to find our way, with the Spirit's help, into the abundance of life that has been offered us by the creative, incarnating Word.[35] Prayer would mean receiving at God's hands, and as a second chance, the life that we had once refused. Prayer would mean consecrated worldliness.

God, you so loved the world that you gave us Jesus Christ to bring to us a ministry of wedding banquets, new wine, and children playing at weddings in the market place. We ask you to help us today to understand the side of discipleship that is passionate, sensuous, and revelling in love.

We realize how easily we mortify the flesh in order to parade our meagre, carefully calculated morality. . . .

Give us, we pray, the mind and energy of Paul who . . . says, "I can do all things (through Christ) who strengthens me" [36]

Chapter 4

Prayer as Representation

"Seek the welfare of the city where I have sent you into exile, and pray to the LORD on its behalf. . . " (Jeremiah 29:7).

. . . I urge that supplications, prayers, intercessions, and thanksgivings be made for all men. . . . This is good, and it is acceptable in the sight of God our Savior, who desires all men to be saved and to come to the knowledge of the truth (Timothy 2:1,3-4).

Elect—Not Elite

Prayer means becoming worldly, tasting the abundance of the life God created, making good our earthly citizenship. Yes, but not just for ourselves!

As noted in the Introduction, self-improvement is a poor motivation for any follower of the One who came to deliver us from preoccupation with ourselves. This deliverance makes us capable of turning in love towards God and our neighbor. It may be a very commendable thing if persons, through grace, lose their primitive and sinful anxiety about life and discover something of the wonder and glory of God's good world—the "banquet" of existence. But is that where the story ends—with a few believers who have found their way into the world and who, through prayer, are going from one stage of sanctified worldliness to the next?

By no means! It would be a truncated version of the Christian life if that were believed. The church is not an elite, but a body of the elect. There is a world of difference between the two concepts. Though both assume a minority status, the purpose of the minority is very different in elitist thinking from what it is in the biblical concept of divine election. In religious and political ideologies that celebrate an elite, "the few" are those golden ones refined out of the great, leaden masses of humanity. The elite do, in this case, constitute the end of the matter—as in the idea of the truly spiritual people (*pneumatikoi*) referred to in the previous chapter. But while the Bible, too, assumes that there will probably only be a few who believe and bear consistent witness to God's truth, these few "chosen" ones are by no means the last word. Not only are they cautioned again and again to refrain from any sort of pride in their election (for "the last will be first, and the first last"—Matthew 20:16), but they also are to know themselves to be nothing more than media in the service of an infinitely greater cause. They are mere "earthen vessels" for transporting a treasure far more precious than anything they could call their own. They constitute, in fact, only a means to a much broader end. This end is so broad, so inclusive, that the writers of the Epistles (often quoting the Old Testament) can only employ the word "all" to signify it—as the author of First Timothy does in the quotation heading this chapter. The writer of Hebrews, quoting Jeremiah 31:31-34, expresses the logic of election succinctly when he writes concerning its goal:

> And they shall not teach every one
>   his fellow
> or every one his brother, saying,
> 'Know the Lord,'
> for all shall know me,
> from the least of them to the
> greatest.   —Hebrews 8:11[37]

In short, the elect are elected to a purpose and a mission, not to a status. They are called to be something ("yeast," "salt," "light," and so forth) in and for the world. The purpose of their own conversion to life is to equip them for God's kingdom-building work in the world at large. The personal turning of the elect towards the world, towards creation, towards "burning Rome" is only the beginning of the affair. It would be a theoretical beginning indeed if they were not thrust by God's persistent and yearning love into a new identification with and commitment to the other human beings, collectivities, and species that are the living constituents of the world.

Being There for Others

The traditional way of speaking about all this is to say that the people of God are a priestly people, and that prayer, therefore, is a priestly act. We cannot allow ourselves to dispense with the symbol of the priest, regardless of our denominational heritage, for it is deeply rooted in our most important doctrinal sources, including the Scriptures. Both the testaments express the meaning and vocation of the elect of God in the language of priesthood. The author of First Peter, quoting Exodus chapter 19, states:

> But you are a chosen race, a royal priesthood, a holy nation, God's own people, that you may declare the wonderful deeds of him who called you out of darkness into his marvelous light. Once you were no people but now you are God's people; once you had not received mercy but now you have received mercy (1 Peter 2:9-10).

The Abrahamic covenant already anticipates this priestly self-understanding of those with whom God enters into a special relationship and agreement: "I will bless you, and make your name great, so that you will be a blessing. . . and by you all the families of the earth will bless themselves" (Genesis 12:2-3). A priest is one who is there for others, not for himself or herself alone.

Unfortunately, however, the concept of priesthood has been marred, or at least rendered ambiguous, by Christian history. This has happened because priests themselves and the priestly class have often contradicted, in their behavior if not in their theory, the very reason for their existence. They have fostered the notion of priesthood or ordained ministry as a special status, elevated above the laity either sacramentally or professionally or both. The Reformation, as well as many attempts at reform in Catholic tradition, tried to correct this misappropriation of the biblical conception of priesthood. The Reformers, as is well known, spoke of "the priesthood of all believers." But even this and other radical theological rethinking has not liberated the theology of priesthood from cooptation by an essentially elitist bias. With the Reformation's official rejection of priestly orders in favor of a priestly or ministerial office and the priesthood of all believers, one had the emergence on the one hand of a new professionalism (the educated clergy) and on the other of Christian individualism, which interpreted the priesthood of all believers to mean: "I don't need any priest, thank you; I am my own priest!"

This is entirely germane to our subject because religious as well as social custom has habitually made prayer the priest's special privilege and talent. Hence, in both Catholic and Protestant circles the perpetuation of a priestly elite has gone hand in hand with a theology of prayer that excludes the full participation of the laity and fails, therefore, to explore the corporate nature of prayer.

Without discarding the concept of priesthood, then, but through repeated attempts to reclaim the plenitude of its biblical significance, we need to discover alternative ways of explaining what it connotes and what meaning it has for the theology of worship. As suggested previously, the biblical metaphor of the steward, which for other reasons has acquired genuinely symbolic status in our time, could help to achieve this.[38] But whatever the specific language we employ, the basic thought—if we are to be true to the biblical theology of priesthood—must express the idea of representation.

When as a worshipping congregation, as two or three gathered together, or even as individuals in our solitude, we come before God in prayer, we do not come only as private persons or as a fellowship of believers set apart from the unbelieving world. We come, rather, as persons whose lives have been sufficiently liberated from purely personal pursuits and cares to be enabled to identify ourselves in a profound way with others. Having begun our spiritual journey into the interior of God's beloved world; having encountered there many human and nonhuman creatures in great need; and having known ourselves to be undeservedly befriended by a healing Spirit, we have begun to learn the sort of compassion and service that enables us now, in worship, to bring these others before God. We represent them.

Representation is not only a matter of remembering the others, as well-known forms of prayer so often state the matter ("We remember before you, our Father, the poor and destitute, the hungry, travellers at sea . . . and so forth"). It is, rather, as if those others were actually present with and in us, as if they had become part of us and we of them; so that their hurts and longings were ours. The usual remembering that is associated with prayers of intercession is no great feat of the human spirit. It can be done with the least inconvenience, and thousands of Christians do it daily, repeating names and facts as effortlessly as superstitious medieval Christians repeated their formulae, their Hail Mary's and Our Father's. It is something else when those for whom we pray are those with whom our lives have become inextricably commingled.

An illustration from South and Central American experience today may help to establish the point. In many Christian ceremonies, when the names of those who have disappeared or have been killed by the ubiquitous death squads are called out, the congregation responds vigorously, "Presento!" The absent ones are present in the *corpus Christi*, the body of Christ, bruised and humiliated as of old.

Our High Priest, Our Representative

The classical illustration of what representation means is of course the New Testament's picture of Jesus in the Garden of Gethsemane—the cross before the cross, as it has often been called. It is a misleading interpretation of this central moment in the life of our Lord when (no doubt well-meaning) piety makes it appear that Christ's suffering and agony were from a personal fear or abhorrence of what was to happen. Such an interpretation is usually part of a misguided attempt to demonstrate that he suffered more than anyone ever has, thus distancing him from the rest of us even in his suffering and death—which is where he in fact comes closest to us. Of course Jesus' agony is also personal. He was fully human, not above fear and even terror. He did not court death, because his mission was life. He was a Jew, and therefore he did not consider death a release or in any way desirable. He was against death. *Jesus Christ Superstar* understood all this better than much theology and Christian piety.

But the point is that Jesus here in Gethsemsane is no lone individual facing a bitter tomorrow. Who among us is ever an individual, really? We all "cast shadows not our own." But he, faith declares, is in a unique sense more-than-individual. He is Humanity, *vere homo* ("truly human") as the Chalcedonian Christology insisted. He is not just a man, but *the* man, as Luther put it in his famous Reformation hymn, "A Mighty Fortress Is Our God:"

> But for us fights the proper man
> The man of God's own choosing.

He is not a superman, nor is he a god, though in the history of mythology and religion such figures are common. "*Ecce, homo!*" ("Behold, the man") cries his judge, that same Pilate who asked cynically what truth might be (see John 19:5). Such a statement held high symbolic significance for the early and medieval church, and was a favorite subject of Christian art. He is the proper man, and therefore it belongs to his humanity, inspired by deity, to be there on behalf of all the others; to be "the man for others" (Bonhoeffer). When he prays in Gethsemane, while his prematurely weary and irresolute disciples sleep, he prays for all. It is Jesus' high-priestly prayer. Jesus has entered so far into the dark interior of God's beloved world, has become so bound up with its pathos, has longed so fervently for its *shalom*, that all the agony of a mother for her failing child is contained in his prayer. After Gethsemane, the cross as such is nothing more—nor less—than the final enactment of this suffering love, this *agape*, which has its basis in the Christ's identification with suffering creation. If that cross is the final representational enactment of that love, its beginning goes far back beyond the birth at Bethlehem to the very origins of the human failure to rejoice in our creaturehood. It goes back to that original sin that looked to the serpent, to forbidden fruit, to whatever it vainly imagined as something better. The love that finally laid down its life for its friends had been journeying towards Golgotha for a very long time.

It is precisely this final enactment of the representational agape of God into which, through baptism and Eucharist, through the Spirit, through preaching, and through prayer, as Christians we are carried—no doubt like Peter, "where [we] do not wish to go" (John 21:18). Our existence as church, as the ones "called out"— the summoned ones (*ekklesia*)—is our incorporation into this representative life of Jesus our High Priest. Our discipleship is our participation in his vicarious suffering with and for the world. Our prayer, then, when it is real, is always a sacramental reenactment of Gethsemane.

Existential Proximity

But there is a condition for this priestly act of the church. It is the same condition that Jesus himself had to meet. Like him and through him, we, too, must achieve an existential proximity to those for whom we pray.

"Existential" is an overworked and still somewhat obscure adjective. It is hard to avoid it, however, in this particular connection. What Jesus achieved, according to the scriptural record of his life and passion, was an existential proximity to God's beloved world. We are all in proximity to the world simply by being here. But his closeness to the world was something else.

It was, in effect, the opposite of theoretical closeness. Many people seem to be able to be in the world without being touched by it or touching it. Every morning on my way to the university where I work, I pass through a section of the city that has the reputation (perhaps undeserved) for being the essence of WASPness. The well-mannered, well-dressed citizens of this affluent area seem wonderfully agile—they are able to make their way to the back of the crowded morning bus with an absolute minimum of body contact.

Jesus, pressed by throngs, touched by suffering women, surrounded by children, embraced by men, was evidently not so adept at reserving space for himself!

How can one treat such a figure theoretically? Christologically? The same people who are able to move through crowded buses without being jostled seem able to speak and think and write about the incarnation, cross, and resurrection as if dealing with theory. With some objectivity they point to the *Logos* of God becoming flesh; the second Person of the Trinity suffering for the world's sins; the victim becoming the victor, and so forth. The formula is satisfying; it has a certain theoretical balance to it—after hundreds of years of such theory, that is, and provided you accept the basic premises.

In the process, however, truth is reduced to doctrine, and at the level of ordinary church life, this allows congregations to pray about terrible suffering in the world without feeling very much, if any, pain in the process. There is no bodily contact. Having lifted up their polite collects and petitions for the poor black people in South Africa or the children of Ethiopia or the oppressed peoples of Central America and Afghanistan, they greet one another at the coffee hour after the service as though they had never shared these terrible thoughts. I should say *we* greet one another so—for I, like Isaiah, "am a man of unclean lips . . ." (Isaiah 1:5). Truly, one does not notice very much perspiration on us North Americans at prayer, let alone sweat like great drops of blood falling to the ground.

Existential proximity to those whom we intend to represent in our worship means the antithesis of "hit and run" praying. God will not hear prayer that is painless, that causes no inconvenience to its authors, that involves no bodily contact. We are responsible for those for whom we pray. We respond to God for them and we become God's response to them. It is not a matter of turning the whole thing back to God. Representational prayer means the realization of our solidarity with the world—especially with its victims—and the acceptance of a new responsibility for it and for them. Therefore, to pray is to announce to God and to one another our readiness to accept God's invitation to participate in the vicarious life of the Christ, to become in deed as well as in thought and word his Body, and to extend his priesthood in and for the world. It is an awesome thing, and not to be entered into lightly.

The Sacrifice of Prayer

Prayer carries a cost. Here we see the inevitable and inescapable, if paradoxical, connection between the joy and the burden of the life of contemplation and prayer. The two things are inseparable: You cannot have the joy without bearing the burden; and if you bear that burden you will know the joy, for in spite of everything this burden is light.

The Christian life begins with joy, the blessedness—often the pure happiness—of discovering God's world and our own right place within it. It is the joy of belonging. It is the joy of becoming who we are; of not having to be gods any longer; of not having to be mere animals either. It is the *joie de vivre*—liberation for truly human life.

But this same joy of life soon leads us down a pathway that this world's devotees of the pleasure principle cannot find very enticing. Once you begin to love the world the future of the world begins to matter. It is no longer only your own future and that of your intimates that matters. You have been embraced by a love that in turn impels you to embrace all. "To the Christian . . . it is of vital importance, it is a matter of life and death, that the world should succeed in its enterprise, even its temporal enterprise."[39] Mere hedonism is incapable of the burden of those who care. But hedonism is also incapable of the joy that is given to the bearers of the

burdens of the world. Only those who lose their lives really find
life (see Luke 17:33).

Yet we should not mistake the prerequisite. There is a sacrifice
involved in this love.

> The man who has determined to admit love of the world and its cares
> into his interior life finds that he has to accept a supreme renuncia-
> tion. He has sworn to seek for himself outside himself, in other
> words to love the world better than himself. He will now have to
> realize what this noble ambition will cost him. . . .
>
> The world, and subjection to the world, and the duty of serving the
> world, are hard to bear, like a cross; and it was to force us to believe
> this that Christ wished, overlooking all the highways of the earth, to
> rise up in the form of the crucifix, the symbol in which every man
> could recognize his own true image.[40]

Lest someone think that the reference here is only to a sort of
emotional or poetic identification with the world, its victims, and
its fate, let me hasten to insert that the kind of existential proximity
that I mean here has a good deal to do with the mind as well as the
heart and the body. It is not merely theory! But then, the mind is
capable of more than theory.

The basic hypothesis of this brief exercise in in the theology of
prayer is that prayer in the name of Jesus Christ means thinking our
way into God's world. When it comes to the responsible representation of our world in prayer, the saying is true that "tears are not
enough." It requires also knowledge, wisdom, discernment,
awareness, research, and disciplined, vigilant study. The life of
prayer and the life of discernment and study are not two different
lives, alternatives from which the elect are free to choose. They are
part of the same life process, the unceasing prayer of thinking our
way into God's world.

To be direct for a moment: How much do you really know
about Central America? Have you ever been to Nicaragua? Have
you listened with an open mind to some of the many groups of
Christians in North America who have been there? Or have you

only heard, with half an ear, the television reports about that country? What sort of study have you undertaken—perhaps with other people in your congregation—about the various aspects of the environmental crisis, the rapid disappearance of various species of animals, the pollution of freshwater systems, the threat to the ozone layer of our atmosphere, and so forth? How many unemployed persons, suicidal youths, battered mothers and children, raped women, depressed and unwanted senior citizens, failed athletes and artists, unsuccessful small business people, and so forth have you actually come close to?

By the time Jesus took a few of his sleepy and uncomprehending followers into that dark and secluded garden—the New Testament's counterpart of Eden—he had achieved existential proximity to a great many oppressed, sick and discouraged persons, as well as naked exposure to the political and religious systems that were responsible for their oppression, sickness, and discouragement. He did not go to that garden of sorrows straight from some living room with matching furniture and wall-to-wall carpeting. He had spent a lifetime with the sick and maimed and blind, with those with leprosy, with fallen women, with dispirited cynical men, with self-righteous leaders and people who wanted, above all, to maintain the status quo. He had made his bed with sinners and outcasts. He had accompanied at table and elsewhere disreputable persons, making it almost impossible for the reputable people to show him any respect publicly. If they wanted to see him, they had to come at night. He had gone to the very heart of this world's darkness. Finally, he had to go still farther, to the hell of forsakenness, dying young, unbefriended, unmarried, unfulfilled, and unsuccessful.

Only in this way had he earned the right and possibility of priesthood.

We do not have to go so far. For one thing, we couldn't take it. For another, we ourselves are as much in need of being befriended by such a priest as are those whom we are called to represent. But costly grace does not mean that we can simply sit by and let Jesus do it all, over and over again.

Must Jesus bear the cross alone,
And all the world go free?

So many of our prayers sound as if the answer we should like to give to the old gospel hymn was "Yes, go to the widow and the orphan once more, Jesus, to the dying children, to the anxious rich—go to all of them, so that we can have our coffee afterwards with peace of mind!"

No; there's a cross for every one,
And there's a cross for me.

Truly, we do not have to bear the great cross. Only "the man of God's own choosing" can bear the cross of Golgotha. But we do have to stand in the environs of Golgotha; and that, in our present context, means that prayer for the world, its victims, and its fate will be legitimate in our case only where it has been preceded and will be succeeded by a good deal of effort to understand and stand with those for whom we pray.

Once when I attended a large prayer conference as one of its invited speakers, I found myself ensconced in a posh automobile owned by one of the organizers, being transported with some of the other speakers to one of the sessions of the conference. Before we had left the parking lot, the driver begged us to be quiet for a moment—not for the purpose of silent meditation, but in order that she might be able to hear on her car radio how her stocks were doing. The stocks in question turned out to be doing very well indeed. They were investments in a multinational corporation specializing in the manufacture of armaments.

The Word whose enfleshment entailed the most excruciating journey towards this world intends to lead his Body, the church, so far as possible to that same core of planetary darkness—to the place where life and death still struggle with one another. No one really is ever prepared for such a journey, but those who sense no discrepancy between the economics of armaments and prayer in the name of the crucified Christ are not even ready to leave the parking lot.

Prayer Can Be Dangerous

What might it mean, though, if even a small fraction of those on this continent who announce their faith in Jesus really accepted the invitation to undertake such a journey to the interior? What could it mean if, when they prayed in their churches and centers of Christian education, a significant minority of Christians in North America really had achieved existential proximity to the Third World? What might it mean if they actually prayed for the ones whom our media insist on naming "the enemy"? What if they prayed for them, really knowing something about them, perhaps even knowing some of the human beings in question? What changes might be brought about in the world situation, in our social attitudes, perhaps even in the policies of our governments, if the prayers of congregations in several American and Canadian cities began to be "priestly"? Could we come away from those moments before God, with Christ in Gethsemane, ready for the predictable joviality (and superficiality) of the coffee hour? Could we come away just as unconcerned as we were beforehand about those for whom we had prayed: the unemployed, the homeless, the poor, the vanishing animal and plant species, the future generations whose destiny is being decided in the boardrooms of multinationals? Could we be, as we often are now, even less concerned than we had been before, knowing that the whole thing had been taken to the Lord in prayer?

Real prayer can be dangerous. It can carry us, in spite of ourselves, into the marketplace and out along the highways of this world. In the ditches beside those highways there are many who have fallen among thieves. For significant numbers of them, we are the thieves, and they will recognize us as such. Can thieves be priests?

Priests who pass by on the other side are only priests in name.

Praying, Thinking, and Acting Justly

Part II

Chapter 5

False Divisions

"If you know these things, blessed are you if you do them"
(John 13:17).

The Nature of Prayer

What are we doing when we pray?

One facet of this question has led us to consider prayer in relation to the life of the Christian community as it moves within the larger human community. Prompted by Karl Marx's critique of religion as the people's opiate, we asked whether Christian prayer, as the most intimate aspect of the interior life of the *koinonia,* is an escape-hatch from an incendiary world or a doorway into it. Our response has necessarily involved us in a wide-ranging consideration of the character of the Christian life and mission. While whose who pray in the name of Jesus Christ recognize the need to stand apart from the world in order to gain perspective on its often chaotic and almost always confusing movement, prayer has as its end a more intensive involvement with the world, not withdrawal from it. With and in the One who wills to transform this world, the community of the cross achieves a solidarity with the real world through prayer that it could never attain apart from courage that comes by faith. In this way, the community's life of contemplation and devotion is the mode of its own entry into the heart of God's good earth, and also a vital mode of its representational (priestly) identification with suffering humanity and groaning creation.

The question, What is prayer? contains another kind of concern. This concern is related to but also different from the consideration of prayer as a function of the witnessing community within the life of the world. If one asks, "What are we doing when we pray?" one can be asking about the purpose of prayer. However, one also can be asking about the nature of prayer.

There is a very fine line of distinction between nature and purpose, but I take nature here to mean the character of prayer itself and as such, rather than its place and function within the life of the believing community. Possibly we should have reversed the order of our reflections and considered the nature of prayer before thinking about its larger purpose. However, it seemed better that we first clarify why we pray to begin with. We need to remind ourselves of the greater context and office of prayer, so that when we come to the question of the nature of prayer we would be guided by a renewed understanding of its function in the Christian life. Our main thesis is that prayer is a matter of thinking our way into God's world, and there can be no question but that the final phrase of that statement is the key so far as the telos (inner aim and end) of prayer is concerned.

But the first part of the statement is also important and perhaps provocative; and now that we have asked about the goal of prayer we are in a better position to ask about the means by which this goal is attained. Thinking!

This is where we approach more explicitly the question of prayer's nature. One way of discussing the nature of anything is by considering it in relation to other entities or realities to which it is connected and from which it is also differentiated. What is the relation between praying and thinking? Then we should go on and ask about the relation between praying, thinking, and acting. For all three are aspects of what Christians mean when they speak about discipleship, obedience, and all the related subjects.

There is a splendid story in Second Kings about the prophet Elisha and the Shunammite woman. In the story, a wealthy woman has her husband add a chamber to their home so that Elisha, whom she perceived to be a holy man, could stay there whenever he chose (2 Kings 4:9-10).

When Elisha asked what he, in turn, could do for this generous woman, he learned that her great sorrow was that she had no child. Elisha promptly promised that she should have a son—and she gave birth to a son "the following spring" (4:17).

The boy grew to adolescence, but one day he developed a headache while out in the field with his father. His father immediately took him home but he died shortly thereafter on the lap of his grieving mother. So tentative seem the promises of God! A son is born after much longing. The son flourishes. The son dies. It is a familiar paradigm, for it is the Bible's way of speaking about grace, which is never simple, straightforward, or predictable.

After searching for the holy man, the Shunammite woman easily persuaded him and he came to the place where the dead boy lay.

When Elisha came into the house, he saw the child lying dead on his bed. So he went in and shut the door upon the two of them, and prayed to the LORD. Then he went up and lay upon the child, putting his mouth upon his mouth, his eyes upon his eyes, and his hands upon his hands; and as he stretched himself upon him, the flesh of the child became warm. Then he got up again, and walked once to and fro in the house, and went up, and stretched himself upon him; the child sneezed seven times, and the child opened his eyes. Then he summoned Gehazi and said, "Call this Shunammite." So he called her. And when she came to him, he said, "Take up your son." She came and fell at his feet, bowing to the ground; then she took up her son and went out (2 Kings 4:32-37).

Like all good stories, this one contains many nuances of meaning. The parallel with a number of the healing incidents in the ministry of Jesus, for one thing, is unmistakable. But more importantly, as seen in the verbatim quote from the Revised Standard Version, prayer, thought, and act are all combined in a single process. The prophet prays, as noted in verse 33. The prophet thinks, meditating in an intense way as he walks "to and fro" in the room. The prophet acts—very physically, in fact—as God did when God created the human pair, as Jesus did when he healed a blind man (Mark 8:23). What is most noteworthy, however, is that the three movements of the healer-prophet are inseparable and almost entirely indistinguishable aspects of the single work of healing and mercy.

I should like to demonstrate in this second part of our study that praying, thinking and acting *justly,* (as Bonhoeffer correctly phrased it[41]), are components of the same process in the life of the Christian and the Christian community. If prayer is indeed a matter of thinking our way into God's world, then thought that did not issue in an active engagement with the world would be a very questionable form of thought. Similarly, an act that did not presuppose and entail a high degree of serious and prayerful thinking would be equally dubious if prayer means thinking our way into God's world.

We cannot, however, ignore the fact that precisely such divisions surround this entire subject. Therefore, before we attempt to expand on the connectedness and interaction between prayer, thought, and deed, we should reflect briefly on the character of the misunderstandings which, all to consistently, inform the life of the ecumenical church and of our whole social milieu with respect to this subject.

The false divisions that I want to treat are, accordingly, the division between praying and thinking, and the division between all forms of thought (including prayer) and act. We shall consider them in that order. It should be remembered, however, that they are not really two distinct divisions, but part of the same divisiveness, and as such a dimension of what both theologians and social theorists have named the "alienation" that is typical of our age.

Mindless Prayer

The division between prayer and thought can be observed by anyone who looks for it. It is present in every Christian community known to me. It is not to be equated with the distinction between Christian communities that place a high degree of value on thinking (such as seminaries or schools of theology) and those whose membership is less intellectually occupied. Whenever we discuss a subject like this, we should avoid the temptation to assume that thought is by and large limited to persons who have been professionally trained to think. Universities and theological schools have no monopoly on thought. There are very thoughtful Christians who have never looked inside a university. Conversely, alas, there are theological students and teachers who are, despite their learning, rather thoughtless people. Let it be clear that we are not speaking here about a division between Christian intellectuals and "ordinary" Christians.

Christian persons who try to be thinking people, whether professional or lay, very often have a critical regard for prayer—amounting sometimes to a very low opinion indeed. There are both reasonable and unreasonable causes for such an attitude. In the succeeding chapter we shall examine in greater detail what has happened to the concept of thinking in our epoch to distinguish it, rather questionably, from prayer. For the present, we are going to concentrate on the causes of the division in question that stem from the truncation—not to say trivialization—of prayer.

The "thinkers" in the churches are frequently lukewarm or skeptical about prayer because they are reacting to what prayer seems to have come to mean. After all, phenomena of every sort are defined, or at least highly colored, by their actual instances; and what is prominently instanced as prayer in the North American religious scene today appears to many people both inside and outside the churches as conspicuously mindless.

In certain ecclesiastical circles, prayer appears to be genuine only where it is the consequence of a kind of stream-of-consciousness verbal outflow, often verbose in the extreme, and lacking in any kind of nuance, subtlety, insight, or forethought. Stock phrases are thrown in, seemingly at random, to keep the flow going. Because, apparently, the flow itself is what is important in these circles. The tone of voice, the facial expressions, the emotional involvement (characteristically a religious adaptation of country and western music)[42] all appear infinitely more significant than what is actually being said. In fact, a careful analysis of the content of such prayer, where it yielded anything substantive at all, might well show a significant level of the presence of hidden persuaders for social, economic, and political convictions of a very doubtful character.

In all probability, readers of this book will immediately be able to picture the type of prayer to which I am referring, for it is in fact the most visible type in our society, where so-called "evangelism" has become normative Christianity for all intents and purposes. For one thing, the primary medium of communication today is one that favors the visible, gives priority to what is emotionally engaging, and militates against the expression of more complex ideas. Colorful pray-ers, it seems, are very good television entertainment, to say nothing of their appeal to the popular religious imagination.

At the same time, I would caution the reader not to leap to the conclusion that I am referring exclusively to the electronic church and other types of pop-Christianity when I write about the lack of thought by which much prayer seems characterized. Thought-less prayers are offered up regularly in the older and more established denominations of Christendom as well. It would no doubt be unkind (though not untrue) to note that the chief distinction between the prayers of the religious television entertainers and those of many congregational leaders in our mainstream denominations may be nothing more than that their thoughtlessness is couched in different linguistic forms. The one form appeals to one segment of society and the other to another segment. The same point is made from another angle if we consider the fate of truly serious thought in our churches. It is not uncommon, especially in churches with a nonliturgical tradition, that ministers or lay leaders of worship who actually prepare their prayers and offer them as carefully crafted pieces in worship are criticized by their people. Their lack of spontaneity and informality in prayer is received as a mark of insufficient spirituality, or is thought to be condescending or academic. Preparing sermons is one thing but written and read prayers seem a positive scandal to many good Protestants. Apparently the important thing in prayer is not thought, but sincerity. And sincerity, it appears, is not available in one's study at the typewriter, but only on Sunday morning at eleven, in the midst of the congregation, on the spot. This instant sincerity, the quintessence of "good" prayers, is apparently measured by standards of excellence completely different from those that have application to the things of the mind. Indeed, one could easily form the impression that what many people mean when they speak about the sincerity of the clergyperson is more closely related to the lack of intellectual sophistication than to anything resembling wisdom, discernment, and perspective.

Given such a background of ecclesiastical preference and practice, it is not surprising that persons in and around the churches who regard themselves as thinking people are often found to have a low opinion of prayer. Prayer, it seems to them, is what you do when you turn off your mind and just let go. Prayer is faith at its most uncouth—for faith, too, for such critics, often appears to connote the victory of the irrational or transrational, if not reason's actual displacement.

Faithless Thought

But if thinkers tend to consider prayer a rather mindless activity, the reverse is also true. Those most given to prayer are apt to regard the thinkers as persons deficient in faith. Again, we ought to recognize that there are certain legitimate reasons for such an opinion.

There is a good deal of prejudice in it, too, as there is in the former position. However, there are at least some understandable reasons why intellectuals, whether professional or lay, appear to other Christians to be lacking in spirituality. This is especially the case in the classical Protestant denominations. We have always put a good deal of stress upon the importance of knowing. One should know one's doctrine, Bible, and church history. One's faith should be intelligible and communicable. However, by reading the works of Protestant scholars and listening to Christian intellectuals of this or that station, one could conclude that while human beings are not saved by good works, they are saved by good thinking. A certain hierarchy of worth inheres in the very structure of theological education and the authority patterns of the churches. This may be partially an inevitable feature of the training of clergy and theological scholars (though it seems to me more nearly a result of too little education than of too much). Those students for ministry who excel in the various disciplines in their seminaries and graduate schools are rewarded, not only with higher grades and standing within the theological institutions themselves, but often with more prestigious offices and pulpits in the churches. The clergy, not so much through their ordination (in Protestant denominations) as through the professional training that is the condition for their ordination, often appear to the average layperson to be the real Christians because they are more knowledgeable about the faith. The expression "I am only a layman/woman," is still heard far too frequently for us to suppose that this attitude has been replaced by the more recent democratization of the churches.

At the same time, while overtly observing the super-Christianity of the clergy, the laity (and especially the more committed of the laity) frequently harbor a secret suspicion that these highly educated clerics, while rich in knowledge, are poor in faith. Moreover, it is a well-rehearsed explanation of this situation that the faith these ordained persons once might have possessed was dislodged by the gradual but decisive inroads of theological scholarship. Their faith was then replaced by ideas that have little to do with the heart and serve only to separate their possessors from the people in the pews, for whom such notions are far too airy. There is thus a conspicuous gulf in the churches between those who still represent and respect the office of prayer and those with a reputation for sophistication of thought. There are noteworthy exceptions to this, and such exceptions are often impressive. But, as is usual, the exceptions prove the rule. We are all impressed by the Christian intellectual who is at the same time profoundly and genuinely spiritual. We also are impressed by the devout person whose theological and worldly discourse is well integrated with his or her spirituality. Yet the gap between these two modes of Christian life and work is so common that we have come to expect Christian intellectuals to be deficient in or even scornful of prayer, and those who pray much to be equally ill at ease in the realm of ideas.

The Separation of Thought and Act

The second great dichotomy visible in the church today is the division between thought and act. This division is larger than its manifestation within religious communities; it belongs to our society at large. In a way that was neither so obvious nor so potentially dangerous heretofore, we have become a civilization whose thinkers and principal actors—the intelligentsia and the governing elements—seem deeply alienated from each other. In his well-known study of almost three decades ago entitled *The Two Cultures*,[43] C. P. Snow described the dividing wall of mutual incomprehension between the scientific and the humanistic communities of the West. Scientists, he said, know no history, art, or poetry, and most philosophers and literary scholars could not define the Second Law of Thermodynamics. Though his analysis is still pertinent in many ways, it is not so obvious today that the most deplorable division in our society is between those two particular cultures. In fact, in some ways there have been surprising breakthroughs between the sciences and humanities. Representatives of both disciplines have begun to manifest the kind of concern for the world's future that can be shared even when the languages and methods of the disciplines create or maintain old barriers. All over the world, significant minorities call for more interdisciplinary dialogue, and, despite the propensity of intellectuals to hide in their fields of specialization, there seems to be a more positive response to this call to dialogue than was the case even two decades ago.

It might even be said that where the intellectual community feels a commitment to society today, it has achieved a remarkable synthesis of social analysis. From many different quarters we hear that our civilization faces major crises, in relation to which vast changes in the behavior patterns of the affluent peoples of the North in particular are made mandatory. There is almost a tacit agreement across many disciplines that the greatest threat to the world's future is the presence among us of irrational or uncontrolled forces, particularly a rampant and directionless technology. The only salvation for our civilization would be its acquisition of a social vision compelling enough to provide alternative goals for the future.

Yet even where such an analysis and agreement exists among the thinkers of our culture, there is an accompanying sense of futility that often amounts to fatalism or withdrawal from the public realm. The concerned intellectual encounters opposition to his or her concern everywhere—especially from those elements in society that benefit from the leaderless situation. These same unthinking elements—persons and classes whose thinking confines itself to the immediate situation—frequently rise to the top by a devious logic of opportunism in tandem with the absence of a public-spirited citizenry. Thus we witness a breakdown of communications between those who are best equipped to think about the world and those who act, and whose acts are decisive for its future. This constitutes a truly critical world situation, for it means that the movers and shakers of history are deprived of the best wisdom available to them in a civilization that has become extremely complex and requires expertise at every turn. The wise of the earth are tempted or driven to retire into their disciplines, leaving the world's destiny more and more fearfully in the hands of irrational and self-serving forces.

Thought and Deed in Churches

This general cultural phenomenon naturally manifests itself in the churches as well. Yet the separation of thought and act is not so straightforward in the Christian context, largely because both those who spend their time thinking and those who feel compelled to act are motivated by ethical considerations that cannot be assumed in the society at large. Christian activism is not governed by selfish ends. On the contrary, it is usually engendered by the often frustrated sense that something must be done. In a society that daily courts nuclear disaster, biospheric breakdown, the increase of rule by terror and violence, poverty, hunger, economic injustice, and so forth, the activist who rushes in to prevent disaster can only be respected. In such a world, all mature persons will be activists.

Yet the danger of activism, both in theory and in its present-day reality in Christian circles, is that its impatience with the slower and more painful process of prayerful thought will rob it of the wisdom that it needs if its acts are to be pertinent to the ends it wishes to serve. In some ways it is easier to act than to think. Actions may speak louder than words, but what they say is neither automatically profound nor even clear. Compared with the numbers of persons in the churches who are involved, to one degree or another, in activities concentrated upon social justice, ecology, peace, human rights and other extremely important concerns of our time, there are relatively few who are capable of depicting, both accurately and imaginatively, why these activities must be the concern of Christians, and how that concern might be enacted wisely.

I recently listened to a radio interview with a prominent Christian leader whose commitment to some of the most urgent causes in our violence-prone world is nothing less than admirable. As I listened to him attempt to handle the probing questions of the interviewer, I wondered how many members of the radio audience would ever be persuaded of the urgency of those causes by the somewhat hesitant, often glib, though unquestionably passionate and even right answers he offered.

I also found, however, that that line of reflection has a way of turning one back upon oneself. Why have I—why have so many Christian intellectuals—been content to pursue studies in the quiet atmosphere of academe, while leaving the deeds of Christ's disciples to those busy, often harried persons who are in the forefront of the movement? At least we might have helped them formulate the reasons for their concern and involvement.

The problem, then, is by no means to be laid at the doorstep of the activist. Thinkers, in church as in the world, have a very dubious record where responsibility is concerned. Judging from the performance of the intellectual community, the impulse to act is not contained in the experience of contemplation as such. Plato believed that truth, goodness, and beauty were inseparable: you could not know the truth without being moved to act in accordance with the good. In the Bible, knowing and doing, wisdom and goodness, gospel and law, the indicative and the imperative, are part of the same process. Doing the thing is not a second step but the extension of the first step of believing. One may only be said to know if one has expressed one's knowing in the act. "If you know these things, blessed are you if you do them" (John 13:17). But in spite of this counsel from both of the intellectual-spiritual sources of our civilization, it has seemed and still seems eminently possible for many thinkers to pursue their vocations without a trace of intentionality towards the act. They can even use their exalted quest for truth as a fence to sit upon, as an excuse for avoiding the act.

This, I think, is where prayer must come into the discussion of the relation between thought and deed. By now it will be clear, I hope, that by prayer I do not not mean a restrictively religious activity, but a dimension of spirit that may be brought to the act of thought itself. I have said just now that the impulse to act does not seem to be implicit in the experience of thinking as such since so many thinkers appear able to let their thought alone suffice. Might it not be that real prayer could be that impulse? Could prayer be that necessary goad that pushes our reluctant spirits towards the completion of thought in deed? Could prayer be that impulse that moves our minds from the state of detachment (or research) to the state of existential proximity? Could prayer be that over-and-above that in spite of us will turn data into truth and truth into necessity and necessity into love and love into deed?

I can only hope that the necessary division of the ensuing discussion into stages (chapters) will not betray the basic intention, expressed in this introductory chapter, of keeping thought, prayer, and act together. In the next chapter I shall attempt to speak to the first dichotomy between prayer and thought. In chapter 7 I shall turn to the second aspect of the problem: the separation of thought and deed. The final chapter will consist of a summary of the argument put forward in the book as a whole.

Chapter 6

Praying and Thinking

I will pray with the spirit and I will pray with the mind also; I will sing with the spirit and I will sing with the mind also
(1 Corinthians 14:15).

The Reduction of Reason

Prayer is thinking your way into God's world. Whatever else it may be, praying is a form of thinking. But what is thinking?

A beautiful and provocative motto emerged out of a post-Reformation German pietism: *Denken ist Danken.* Thinking is Thanking. To think is to be grateful—grateful to God, grateful for life, grateful for the world, grateful for the privilege of reflection itself. Conversely, those who are truly thankful are engaged in the most profound form of human thought, even though they may not regard themselves or be regarded by the world as thinkers. This is perhaps the best place for us to begin in our attempt to challenge the false division between prayer and thought.

We are hampered in that attempt by two interrelated factors in modern history. The first is the truncation of thought or reason that occurred in Western civilization from about the fifteenth century onwards. The second is the concommitant reduction of the meaning of faith and all things connected with the life of faith, including prayer. In our quest for a new appreciation for the integration of prayer and thought, we are necessarily drawn into this resumé of modern intellectual history.

From about the end of the Middle Ages onwards, thought suffered what from the standpoint of both of the foundational cultural traditions of Western civilization—both Athens and Jerusalem—can only be described as a curtailment. If one considers the kind of thinking that is present, for example, in the Psalms or Proverbs and in the dialogues of Plato, one realizes that this is thought of a very inclusive, wide-ranging character. Nothing whatsoever was withheld from the inquiring mind. No subject was too difficult at least to contemplate, although the wise ones of both traditions knew full well that understanding is never complete. They knew that it was always a matter of of "standing under" the reality they sought to know. Plato was never heard to say, "Sorry, that isn't my field"—the line that comes automatically to the lips of the modern intellectual. As for the psalmists, they were ready to take on the universe—though modestly, of course, because the whole thing is invested throughout with wonder.

> When I look at thy heavens, the
>   work of thy fingers,
> the moon and the stars which thou hast established;
> what is man that thou are mindful of him,
> and the son of man that thou dost
> care for him?   —Psalm 8:3-4

This feeling for the immense scope of the human mind and imagination persisted throughout most of the history of the Christian movement—through the apostolic period, through the early Greek and Latin theologians, through Augustine, through Anselm and Bonaventura and other medieval thinkers. As we see plainly enough in the works of the psalmist quoted above, it was virtually impossible for all of these figures and their contemporaries to draw a distinct line between thinking and faith. Indeed, many of their works (especially Augustine's *Confessions*) are an intermingling of thinking and praying, which for them was simply a single process of reflection and meditation. Their thought was prayer, and their prayer was thought.

But this changed rather rapidly with the waning of the Middle Ages. In fact, the Middle Ages waned because of this change. The consequences of the change for our present subject are very serious indeed, for what happened was that thinking and praying began to be separated from each other in a quite decisive way.

From the end of the Middle Ages onwards, thought is more and more confined to a specific form of thought called empirical thinking. Empiricism is thought restricting its investigations to matters that can be gleaned from the evidence of the senses and adequately tested, preferably under controlled conditions. Already in the High Middle Ages, the empirical mode of thinking entered the scene of scholastic philosophy/theology and began to occupy the most prominent place. "The beginning of our knowledge is from the senses," ("*Principum cognoscendi est a sensu*") declared the theologians who had come under the influence of a renewed interest in the approach of Aristotle. Accordingly, they began to attempt to base all their reflections about God and the universe upon observations common to universal human experience.

Now this did not mean, at first, that thinkers had to give up thinking about the things of God, as we might imagine from the vantage point of a later age. Thomas Aquinas and his teacher, Albertus Magnus (sometimes called "the father of modern science"), employed empirical method but did not end in empiricism. Not only did they retain the ancient feeling for the continuity of faith and reason, but they also recognized, as believers in Christian revelation, that much if not most of what Christians believe defies submission to the sort of investigation and proof-testing that a strictly empirical approach to truth requires. At the same time, they were well aware of the fact that most of their reflective contemporaries could no longer assume that natural truth and revealed truth were part of an inseparable whole, a seamless robe, so to speak. Therefore, they set out to mend the robe of truth that began to be torn by the intellectual and spiritual pressures of the time.

Thomas's brilliant work remains in a real sense a model for all theology—not in its explicit content so much as in its intent. Thomas knew, as all thoughtful Christians know, that a faith that can no longer engage in dialogue with the keenest thinking of its culture can only end in a parochial form of Christianity, yielding a church living on the edge of the world. The Thomistic synthesis of faith and reason was made possible by Thomas's ability to demonstrate that the conclusions arrived at by a rationality empirical and logical in nature were entirely compatible with the conclusions accepted by faith. What faith believed on the authority of the church could not be attained by means of rational investigation, but neither could it be disproved by reason. On the contrary, reason's own positive conclusions about the nature of things, especially of their Source, served only to buttress the tenets of revealed religion.

This synthesis, however, was only as convincing as human religious and social attitudes would allow it to be, and it did not take very long before there arose in the context of evolving European culture and philosophy a posture that was less willing than thirteenth-century piety had been to accept on faith the revealed truths of religion as if they were easily commensurate with the truths of unaided reason. With the advent of what came to be called nominalism,[44] the split between rationality and belief that Thomas and his colleagues had seemed to overcome became conspicuous. William of Ockham and other leading nominalists, though themselves believers and important theologians of their time, felt that rationality is strictly limited so far as its religious potential is concerned. Belief rests chiefly upon revealed truth; and for Ockham, who for other reasons had broken with the papacy and conventional channels of authority, the authority for revealed truth was the Bible. (It primarily was for this reason that the later Protestant reformers, especially Luther, praised Ockham.)

Within the framework of the late medieval church we already
have the roots of the division between thought and prayer. From
this point onwards, despite countervailing movements, the broad
tendency was for reason to seek its home in a quarter of human
experience quite distant from the abode of the religious impulse
and for religion, consequently, to claim for its territory only those
dimensions of human experience that reason could not master.
With the eighteenth-century Enlightenment, however, reason
seemed ready to take over all of life. The rational approach to
existence became ever more self-confident, so that those most
influenced by the ideals of this "clearing up"[45] (including the formulators of both the French and the American revolutionary phi-
losophies) believed it both possible and necessary to live by reason
alone, thus countering the Reformation's *sola fide*—by faith alone.
Reason, for the Enlightenment mentality, still contained a dimension of depth, however; it was not wholly devoid of the sense of
mystery, reverence, and beauty—as can be seen, for example, in
the writings of Thomas Jefferson. If one visits an eighteenth-
century mansion or public building, one realizes that the thinking
that informs this architecture, with its stately (but often nonfunc-
tional) pillars and curving staircases, was by no means governed by
purely practical reason!

However, the process of narrowing the scope of reason did not
end with the Enlightenment. With the Industrial Revolution and
the increasing power of the natural sciences and technologies, what
began with a concentration upon observable human experience
(*empeiria*) yet remained open to the mystery of experience, was
more and more exclusively devoted to pragmatic ends. True rationality now became thought in the service of human mastery—
mastery over the natural world, over chance. The test of truth was
the power and effectiveness of the ideas and inventions to which
rational activity gave rise. Does it work? Empirical reason had
given way to functional or "technical reason" (Tillich).

The consequence of this curtailment of reason has been that all
human thought that is not capable of subjection to controlled test-

ing or does not product tangible results is regarded as less than serious, less than truly rational. Often it is considered mere opinion, if not sheer superstition or bias. Naturally enough, religious thought has been a special target of those who have been able to represent the purest form of scientific thinking. This is true especially in the English-speaking world, where first empiricism and then technical rationality achieved their greatest success. Until very recently, this has meant a twofold kind of response.

Some Christians and other religious persons among the academically inclined have continued to attempt a reconciliation between faith and reason. They have more or less accepted the conception of rationality put forward by empiricist philosophers and natural scientists and others committed to the modern view, and have attempted to demonstrate the compatibility of religious belief and the scientific world view. Those of us who attended universities and other centers of education in the 1950s will no doubt recall that a familiar dialogue centered around the theme of religion and science. In Anglo-Saxon cultures especially, much academic theology has been given over to the cause of achieving a positive discourse between science and religion with subjects like creation and evolution, miracles, and the gaps in rational-scientific explanations of the world occupying prominent places in the discussions.

The more popular forms of religious faith, however, have taken the opposite approach or have, perhaps, been forced into it. Most nonacademic Christianity, having been turned out of the house of reason, has sought shelter in the soul, the heart, or the emotions. Much of what we already noted in the previous chapter by way of anti-intellectualism in the churches has its explanation here. Both negative and positive factors are at work in this. Negatively speaking, if rationality and its most powerful representatives deny religion a place in the sphere of genuine thought, then religion must locate itself elsewhere. But positive factors have also played their part, for when the reigning forms of rationality exclude from their purview everything except that which can be subjected to laboratory testing and produce visible results, they exclude perhaps 95 percent of human experience. There is, therefore, a fertile field for religion in all that is left out of the investigations of the guardians of rationality.

It remains true, however, that even though religion has continued to exist in the modern world and even occasionally to thrive despite the predictions of the more exultant rationalists of the eighteenth and nineteenth centuries, it has been a religion that from the standpoint of early and medieval Christianity, as well as other premodern faiths, is deprived of discourse with the most rigorous forms of human rationality. Indeed, the mindlessness and irrationality that we noted earlier as being very near the surface in contemporary North American religion is in considerable measure traceable to this very divorce between faith and reason.

The Quest for Transcendence

However, there are new dimensions to be observed in this whole area. In our own historical moment—a time referred to by some contemporary scholars as post-modern—significant minorities everywhere have begun to perceive the modern definition and employment of reason as a reduction. They have seen in this limitation of thought to so-called scientific thinking a deprivation of the human community at large. Even scientists themselves have sensed that narrow, empirical thinking may rob the human community of resources of imagination and courage that are necessary to its well-being if not to its very survival. Scientific theory itself is deprived by the reduction of reason to technical rationality, for the most brilliant scientific thought is never devoid of wonder. Moreover, when science and technology are no longer guided by principles that can be gleaned only from forms of reflection that transcend scientific investigation as such, they are soon at the mercy of forces either inherent in their own pursuits or imposed upon them by self-serving powers and principalities.

An example of both the internal and the external forces to which I am referring is nuclearism. When a society is no longer governed by lively goals and standards derived from systems of meaning and morality deeply embedded in its life and history, then the capacities of its know-how and industry for making and doing are virtually devoid of direction. If modern technology moves effortlessly and without significant opposition wherever its own dynamism takes it; if what can be done will be done, then it is hard to avoid the conclusion that such a society is at the mercy of its own technology. If, besides this internal compulsion of technology to lead where it will, there are powerful agencies and influences that can use the directionless situation to their own advantage, then the prospect that the situation will become a dangerous one is even greater. The escalation in the production of armaments in the contemporary world is due not only to the failure of systems of meaning (including thinking religion) to provide positive guidance to the powers of science and technology, but also to the presence of evil influences that move technique in the direction of its most destructive potentiality. That "nothing equals the perfection of our war machines";[46] that military spending represents the most significant single expenditure of entire empires; that ever more fantastic scenarios of warfare, defense, and survival can be entertained as real possibilities by supposedly sane persons are factors that have persuaded more and more people in the post-modern world that a rationality limiting itself to the perfection of techniques for mastery and the elimination of chance is both a truncated and perilous type of rationality.

The dangerous aspect of thinking that has been deprived of the quality of transcendence is not, however, the only reason why critical minorities have emerged that seek the expansion of our understanding of what it means to think. For decades now—indeed for almost two centuries, if one considers the protest of the Romantic Movement against the spirit of Enlightenment and the Industrial Revolution—there have been prominent attempts within Western culture to broaden our concept of reason. Some of the most provocative thinkers of our own epoch have devoted themselves to the work of preserving or reconstructing forms of thought that can enlarge the human spirit and improve the prospects of a civilization caught in the grips of its own restrictive rationalism. Not only theologians (like Paul Tillich, who distinguished empirical-technical rationalilty from what he called "ontological reason" [thinking-about-being][47]), but also many secular thinkers have urged us to gain or regain images of ourselves as thinking beings whose thought ranges widely over the wealth of human experience and is not confined to the world of fact. Thinking, they have said, is not to be equated with mere calculating.[48] Machines can calculate, but machines cannot think. Thinking involves contemplation, meditation, and rumination. That the human being is, as Aristotle said, "a thinking animal," does not imply only that this creature, among all earth's inhabitants, can add and subtract, make houses and submarines, or conquer space. It means that this creature has a capacity for standing off from itself (the literal meaning of the word "existence"). It can transcend its own here-and-nowness, reflect upon its condition and its relation to its environment, ponder, deliberate, decide, wonder, and so forth. It belongs to this creature not only to be but to know that it is and to meditate on the meaning of its being and of all being.

Perhaps it will now be more obvious why it has been expedient for us to engage in a certain amount of historical reflection. One cannot consider the course of Western intellectual history over the past four or five centuries without suspecting that we may have returned, at long last, to a point where the life of reason and the life of faith can again have meaningful concourse with one another. I do not, of course, mean that we can simply pick up where the Middle Ages left off and behave as if the modern split between reason and faith never occurred. But the alienation that once separated the way of rationality from the way of belief is giving place to a new openness to dialogue, at least on the part of important minorities within our culture. These minorities have traversed the route of secularity, agnosticism, and atheism. They have learned, in the process, to distrust the little god of a human rationality narrowly conceived. They are certainly not ready to return uncritically to pre-modern forms of religion. Nevertheless, they are ready to explore forms of thinking and action that can flow from such thought and contribute to a more thoughtful society. Such a society would be more likely to survive than the technically clever but intellectually and spiritually impoverished civilization that resulted from the divorce of skillful reason from prayerful reason.

The Obligation of Christians to Think Again

There is a new quest for transcendence, a new dimension of spirituality in the thinking of many humanists, scientists, social scientists, artists, writers, and ordinary citizens in our post-modern society. This new spirituality places upon the churches and upon individual Christians an obligation to meet that human quest with understanding and with a willingness to learn from it as well as respond to it. While there are certainly many Christians who are prepared to do just that, there are also barriers to such a dialogue on the Christian side of the divorce.

One of these barriers is the tendency of so much North American Christianity to distrust human thought even when it is more or less friendly towards faith, and to turn belief into credulity.[49] By credulity I mean the unthinking, blind acceptance of dogma. Many of our formerly secular contemporaries have given evidence of a new openness to spirituality in their thinking. But the question for Christians is, are we ready to incorporate more serious thinking into our life of contemplation and prayer?

We began by saying that whatever else it is, prayer is a type of thinking. However, as we noted in the previous chapter, it is unfortunately the case that much prayer seems conspicuously lacking in depth of thought. The world, at least to some of its most sensitive contemporary spokespersons, has begun to recover the prayerful character of all true thought. There is an unmistakable hint of the "thinking is thanking" motif in much secular literature today. Can the church recover with sufficient imagination and consistency to enable it to meet the invitation implicit in this worldly thinking, the thoughtful character of prayer?

In order to do so, it is necessary for more of us Christians to make ourselves vulnerable to the great questions that the responsible scientists and humanitarians of our civilization have not been able to ignore; questions that have caused them to be open to the very spirituality of which we have been thinking. So long as we Christians are insulated from these questions and find refuge from everything that threatens life in our sanctuaries and our dogmas, we shall not be capable of profound thought. Thought occurs when security is no longer a foregone conclusion—when the mind must venture out into unknown places and rethink the answers on which its former security was based.

Isn't that where faith occurs, too? Faith that is not sight but trust, and hope? Does faith not also "see best in the dark" (Kierkegaard)? Is not the language of faith—prayer—precisely an asking for what we do not have, a readiness to entertain consciously the questions, doubts, and uncertainties that are there in us, believing that there is an Answerer, even when there are no answers?

Too many Christians are afraid to think because they fear that thought will destroy their faith. But what kind of faith is it, in that case? What kind of prayer functions to conceal from our minds our deepest thoughts? Prayer is not an alternative to thought—it is thought at its most adventuresome!

When I was an undergraduate student in university, a rather callow and not altogether humble young man (as candidates for ministry sometimes tend to be), I was walking home with an acquaintance of mine who was also a candidate for the ministry of our denomination. This man, famous on the campus for his piety (and his intellectual sloth), suddenly confronted me with the question, "Do you pray?" Taken off guard, and somewhat incensed by the indignity of the question, I replied testily that of course I prayed—I prayed in the library, I prayed in the lecture halls, I prayed all through late-night discussions with my fellow students, I prayed in films and plays, I prayed over my books of biology and literature and Greek—in fact, I said, I did the scriptural thing and prayed quite literally "without ceasing"! The astonished fellow, convinced as he was in advance that such a one as I never prayed at all, was quite overcome.

If he is still in the land of the living, I hope that this gentleman has forgiven a haughty young theologue his self-righteousness. But I also hope that he has learned, in the meantime, something of the truth that lay behind that theologue's impulsive self-defense. Prayer is not a thoughtless alternative to thought; not a warm little spot in the heart or soul where we can have sanctuary from the hard and sometimes searing questions that will take up residence in our heads. It is, rather, a dimension and quality that we are allowed to bring to our thinking. Prayer, at its most authentic as well as its most obedient, means the courage to think (see 2 Samuel 7:27). It is the permission to think about everything, the good and the bad, the joyful and the fearful, the things of which we are proud and the things of which we are deeply ashamed, the secrets of the universe and the secrets of our own hearts. Nothing has to be left out of this thought; everything is permitted because it is thought undertaken in the presence of One who knows our needs before we ask, and whose peace passes understanding.

Where does thought leave off and prayer begin? Who can classify these two movements of the human mind, these ventures in understanding and being understood? Who will say that one thing belongs to prayer, the other to thinking?

Perhaps the most famous graphic portrayal of human thought is Rodin's well-known sculpture, "The Thinker." Everyone knows that this seated figure, with head resting on fist and furrowed brow, is immersed deeply in thought. Yet by the standards of modern rationality the figure seems strangely bereft and incongruous. He has none of the scientific and technical tools of thought—no microscope, sextant, or instruments for measuring and controlling nature. He has no computer. He is, in fact, naked. He is engaged in no activity whatsoever—he just sits there. Yet we know, immediately and intuitively, that he is thinking, and profoundly so. He is lost in thought.

We wonder if he perhaps is praying.

Chapter 7

Thought, Word, and Deed

"Not every one who says to me, 'Lord, Lord,' shall enter the kingdom of heaven, but he who does the will of my Father who is in heaven" (Matthew 7:21).

Just Thinking

Finding precisely the right title for a book is never an easy task. One is almost bound to give some readers and potential readers of one's work a false impression of what it is about, because titles hardly ever contain the whole burden of the message the author wants to communicate. To clarify properly a title, the author would have to emulate those Germanic works of yesteryear, whose titles were often an entire paragraph in length.

The limitation of the title that I have given this book is no doubt obvious. It places a certain accent on the word "thinking," and for many Christians and others that is a word that is suspect from two angles. One angle presents the suspicion that people who emphasize thinking are prone to discount or downplay other forms of human spirituality, including prayer. I hope that I have appeased that suspicion in the previous chapter.

The other angle presents the vantage point of those who fear—with considerable justification—that thinking is often just thinking. Karl Marx was one of them. "The philosophers," he wrote, "tried to understand the world; but the point is, to change it!"[50] Another modern critic of the human condition, Sigmund Freud, was still more devastating. He introduced the term "rationalization," with its implication that much of what we are doing when we say we are thinking is really a matter of covering up or blocking out our subconscious feelings with layers of conscious thought especially manufactured for the purpose.

Even everyday speech is filled with expressions of this suspicion. The dreaming child in school is cautioned to "Stop daydreaming and get to work!" "Actions," we are forever being reminded, "speak louder than words." As a child I remember singing a ditty to my enemies of the moment, in response to their little taunts and insults, which went, "Sticks and stones will break my bones, but words will never hurt me." "Put your money where your mouth is!" "I'm, from Missouri, I have to be shown." "Handsome is as handsome does." An almost limitless supply of such maxims stands ready for our use, especially in the work-oriented and pragmatic society of North America. All of these maxims come down to this: thought is mere window-dressing if it does not issue in deed, and words are not to be construed as deeds.

Those of us who spend our days making words and thinking thoughts are apt to resent all this because we know perfectly well that thinking is hard work. In fact, persons who take their intellectual work seriously are often greatly relieved to have to do physical labor, and many of them elect to spend their leisure hours performing tasks that the average day laborer would regard as too exhausting or boring. Dividing the world into neat categories of thinkers and workers is a rather silly habit.

All the same, we recognize the truth of the complaint that thought is sometimes just thought—that it stops there, producing no corresponding act, inducing no movement of the will, commanding no effort of the body. It would appear that the impulse to act is not contained in thought as such.

If one considers the performance of the Western world's intelligentsia over the past century, one can scarcely avoid such a conclusion. Among the large numbers of intellectuals in German universities in the 1930s, for example, only a handful actively protested against the evolving policies of Hitler's party. In our own situation today, how many intellectuals are really vigilant for the peace and well-being of the world? In the academic communities with which I have been associated for most of my adult life, I have to confess that I find about as much concern for and commitment to the public sphere as among the middle classes in general—which is far too little!

This is lamentable and even tragic because the intellectuals of our world are the only persons who are equipped to understand sufficiently the complexity of contemporary society to offer it the self-knowledge and guidance that it so badly needs. Our world has become extremely complicated technically, sociologically, economically, culturally, and religiously. It requires an enormous effort of mind to grasp even this or that aspect of contemporary society, and to derive the kind of perspective that *wisdom* requires, even greater demands on the intellect must be made. For such an overview depends on the readiness of experts in a large number of fields, over and above their devotion to their own specializations, to commit themselves to interdisciplinary dialogue. Everyone who has had experience with the modern university knows that this latter commitment, on which the survival of civilization may depend, is the most rare and difficult goal for academic communities to achieve. This is partly—as we observed earlier—because thinking persons are frequently discouraged from public involvement by the responses with which their attempts at involvement are met by the unthinking and opportunistic elements within our society. Still, if we cannot even think together, pooling the resources of our various kinds of research, contemplation, and technical know-how, how can we ever come to the point of acting in concert? Thus the question that plagues the thoughts of intellectuals who are committed to the world and to action is whether much if not most of the thinking that occurs in such communities is designed to insulate persons from the real world.

Prayerful Thought Is Never Just Thought

Jesus was no stranger to this propensity of the thinker to rest content in thought. The people he had in mind when he uttered the words of Matthew 7:21, just as when he offered his hearers those stories-with-a-twist like the one told in Matthew 25:31-46, are obviously persons who spend a good deal of their time in explicit religious devotion. "Lord, Lord," is frequently on their lips. They make a point of letting God (and everyone else) know that they are there, with heaven on their minds.

But we should not exaggerate. Jesus is referring here to very good people, persons of high religious motivation, not your average religious bigot or pompously holy type. He is, in fact, addressing all of us who pray or say we are praying. What he has to tell us is plain enough: "You have not really been at prayer if you are just praying. Prayer undertaken in my name can never be just prayer. It may begin with my name, but if it ends there, there is something fundamentally wrong with it. It may begin on your knees with your eyes shut, but if it does not carry you out into the marketplace and give quite definite orders to your hands and feet, then you had better think twice about calling it prayer or using my name. What I prayed there in the garden took me as far into this world as it is possible for anyone to go. No, farther! If you want to use my name in your approach to the holy One, be prepared to be sent off in the same general direction!"

Through prayer we are thinking our way into God's world. "Thinking" is a rather weak word, but we have made it so. It quite rightly arouses the suspicions of many good people, and one should be wary of using it in the title of a book about Christian prayer. However, it is thinking that picks us up and carries us where many of us would prefer not to go—*into God's world.*

As such, it is thinking that is forever incomplete, and knows itself to be incomplete, so long as it is only thought. It is thinking that contains within itself an implicit propulsion into life. It is thinking that must articulate itself in speech and in deed. "For we cannot but speak of what we have seen and heard," declared the apostles to the authorities who warned them to keep silent (Acts 4:20). "For necessity is laid upon me," confesses Paul (1 Corinthians 9:16). Clearly enough Paul, like Jeremiah before him, knows well the cost of the thinking into which faith has thrust him. He knows, too, the overwhelming temptation to be silent. But "necessity (*anangkē*: constraint, compulsion, destiny) is laid upon me. Woe to me if I do not preach the gospel!" (1 Corinthians 9:16). In case we are tempted to think that preaching the gospel is after all only a matter of mere words, hardly deeds, we should remember that for Paul, as for the whole prophetic tradition of Israel, the Word is deed. God's Word is "event"; therefore all who bear witness to this event participate in an activity that is infinitely more costly than mere words that "will never hurt me"!

Why Prayer Is Thought-Issuing-in-Act

There is very good reason why the thought that accompanies the life of faith—prayer—propels us into this world. For it is thought that occurs in a quite specific context. This context is characterized primarily by the presence of another, a second party, namely the Spirit who both initiates our thought and causes us to follow thought through to its logical and ethical conclusion. Thought as such seems, as we said, not to contain this ethical dimension. It would be more accurate to say that, while any profound reflection upon truth does inevitably lead to acting out the truth ("acting justly"—Bonhoeffer), human beings are wonderfully adept at finding reasons why the truth cannot be lived. "What is truth?" we ask with Pilate. "It may be true, but it is not practical," we complain. "It is too idealistic. You can't possibly live that way!"

But "the Spirit helps us in our weakness" (Romans 8:26)—though it is the kind of help that we would often rather do without. For it is help that wrestles with our recalcitrant and reluctant spirits (8:15); help that pushes us past our excuses, rationalizations, and attempts to rest content with the thought alone; help that compels us to translate the thought into witness, word, and deed; help that turns profession into confession.

Prayerful thinking, in other words, is thinking-in-relationship. That is why the Epistles speak so often about "praying in the Spirit" (see Ephesians 6:18). We were reminded earlier that Jesus taught his followers to pray quietly, without ostentation, in the solitude of their rooms. But while prayer is undertaken in solitude, it is never permitted to become mere reverie, soliloquy, or monologue. It is always dialogical. This Other, this prompting, helping Spirit brings to prayer questions, judgments, commands, considerations, and permissions that do not enter human thought normally or naturally, or, if they do, are characteristically shown the exit.

Moreover, the relational nature of the thought that belongs to prayer includes a whole host of beings whose destinies become, in prayer, our responsibility. As we said in the fourth chapter, prayer is representational. When we come before God in spirit and in truth we are there, not only in our own behalf, and not only alone with God, but also as those who represent their neighbors, contemporaries, creaturely environs, and earthly home. In the presence of this Other, we are to hear God's Word for all whom we represent and all who are present in our presence. As a priestly people we are given in this encounter with the Eternal a mission and work that has very concrete application to time. It is certainly a mission and work that is broader in scope than our own lives and the lives of our immediate circle. The things that we are brought to think about, as we "pray in the Holy Spirit" (Jude v. 20) are not strictly personal. It is intended for the human beings whose neighbors God has made us, for the world whose stewards divine grace has constituted us. To store it up, perhaps to hide it as the foolish servant did with his one talent, is to deny the priestly calling of those who pray and to treat the biblical understanding of election as if it were, after all, just another of the world's many versions of an elite. We are to remember that we have been chosen for the dialogue of prayer, not because we are personally more acceptable, receptive, or spiritual than other human beings, but because God wills to address and to save all. Therefore, while the thinking that belongs to the life of discipleship is characterized by a certain privacy, solitude, and modesty, it can only achieve its proper end when it has been transmuted into words and deeds that are beneficial to all God's creatures. What begins in the solitude of our closet is not completed until it has become entirely public. Jesus, our high priest, prayed in the dark secrecy of Gethsemane, somewhat apart even from his own most intimate companions. But what he prayed there was only finished (John 19:30) when he was lifted up to public view. Gethsemane was indeed the cross before the cross. But if Jesus' mission had taken him only so far as that garden of sorrows, if he had not also had to walk through the streets of Jerusalem along the Via Dolorosa to the Place of the Skull, he himself would have been judged out of his own mouth: "Not every one who says to me, 'Lord, Lord,' shall enter the kingdom of heaven, but he who does the will of my Father who is in heaven" (Matthew 7:21). In Gethsemane he asked for, tried to alter, but finally bowed to the will of the Father. On Calvary he acted out that will.

Political Prayer

Here we shall introduce the controversial subject of the political nature of Christian prayer. First-World Christians, secure in our suburban, gentrified, and fully equipped houses and churches endeavor to avoid that topic. We have tried very hard to keep private prayer private. Prayer should concentrate on personal needs—our own and those of our friends. When it ventures out into the larger human and extra-human world, it should incorporate only the most general concerns.

Our clergy are trained to walk a very delicate line between the private and the public in their pastoral prayers. Intuitively, if not by bitter experience, they know that they may pray for peace, but without suggesting any negative criticism of their own nation. They may mention our threatened natural environment, provided they avoid any hint of blame that may offend persons of the managerial class in their congregations. They may lay before God's throne the plight of the poor, the homeless, and the oppressed so long as they resist any rebel spirit that may insinuate that our way of life may be the primary cause of the plight of the poor and needy.

We have expended astonishing amounts of psychic energy and ingenuity to ensure that prayer can be kept private—perhaps even innocuously private. We have been particularly tireless in our efforts to justify this religious personalism scripturally. Did not Jesus command us to go to our closets and pray in secrecy? Did he not also say, "My kingship [kingdom] is not of this world" (John 18:36)? Above all, did he not insist that we "render to Caesar the things that are Caesar's" (Mark 12:17)? Should we not uphold the separation of church and state?

All the while we have the cross as the center of the whole message. Jesus' execution was an entirely public thing. The ministry of Jesus Christ began in the quietest possible way. It started with an obscure birth, a young adulthood about which we know nothing, the selection of a few unprominent persons as followers, the silent performance of kind but unspectacular acts of mercy and healing, the teaching of little flocks gathered on hillsides, quiet suppers with friends, and night walks to a nearby park to be alone to pray.

Suddenly the whole thing bursts onto the stage of public life like a scandal in high places. All at once, everyone who is anyone is implicated: the highest of the priests and elders, the leaders of the nation, the king, and even the Roman tetrarch. They are all present, characteristically distrustful of one another, jealously guarding their power, kowtowing to authority while plotting the downfall of their rivals, lying, cheating, bribing, finding a scapegoat—all the usual things of which an age like ours needs no reminding.

How silently, how silently,
The wondrous gift is given!

What began in silence on a starry night ended in thunder and darkness at noon, with every public person and institution called to judgment. What could be more political! It did not happen in that way simply by accident. Not according to these same Scriptures that we search so diligently in our effort to keep the thing personal. It was meant to go that way, to be carried into the streets, to become a public scandal. The whole movement of the Gospels is towards this exposure, this illumination of our darkness. Who could mistake it? From the beginning of the story one knows that it has to end where it does end, right out in the open. There would have been no reason to write the story down in the first place if it had not ended there.

As it is, this is not just a little, homespun fable about a carpenter's son who made a temporary and on the whole abortive attempt to live an alternative lifestyle; it is the saga of a God who determined to change the world. The change had to occur from within, otherwise it wouldn't be the transformation of what was already there but only its replacement—or its obliteration. The change had to begin in the quietest possible way, right inside the womb of the world, as it were. Eventually it had to break out into the light of day, exposing the evil that had spoiled God's good work of six days, and giving new life to the failing hearts and dry bones of the old Adam and the old Eve.

It is still breaking out. The resurrection, that yet-more-political focus of the story that Christians tell, means that the transfiguring presence of the One who was alone with his Father on the mountain is now loosed upon the world at large. To be sure, his kingdom is not of this world, but it is *for* it. What else could we possibly be thinking of when we pray, as he taught us, "Thy kingdom come . . . on earth as it is in heaven" (Matthew 6:10)? That is hardly a very private sort of prayer.[51] Where might it lead if we were to pray that kind of prayer "in the Spirit"? It could lead us, as it has led countless others before us, into public places that so many of our more lovely prayers seem designed to keep us out of. It could lead us to conflict with the powers-that-be, to visions that might shock our well-mannered neighbors and friends, to suffering that we ourselves would do anything to avoid—that we thought religion was meant to help us avoid!

There is in fact no telling where the thinking that begins, innocently enough, in the solitude of our closets and "in the Spirit" may end. But this we may be sure of: it will not end in thought alone.

Chapter 8

Are There Inappropriate Prayers?

"When you spread forth your hands,
    I will hide my eyes from you;
even though you make many prayers,
    I will not listen;
your hands are full of blood."
                            —Isaiah 1:15

. . . for we do not know how to pray
as we ought. . . (Romans 8:26).

Recapitulation—By Way of Negation

At first glance, the question posed by the heading of this chapter may seem an impertinent one. Who is so wise and so righteous as to be in a position to determine whether the prayers of his or her neighbors are appropriate or not? God alone is able to judge such things.

Let it be made clear at the outset, then, that we are not asking here about any specific prayers or the devotional habits of any person or groups of persons. We are asking a theological question, and our purpose in doing so is to express more pointedly some of the concerns that have been aired already in these pages. By saying what kind of prayer would not seem to be consistent with the theology of prayer articulated here (the *via negativa* again), we shall be offering what amounts to a kind of recapitulation of the position taken throughout this study.

As for the actual prayers of real persons we neither can nor wish to pass judgment. No one who has a familiarity with the Scriptures would want to suggest that God rejects, in advance, the sincere prayers of any human being. It belongs to the freedom of our relation with God that we may be entirely honest—at least as forthright and open as we are in our most intimate human relationships. "Have no anxiety about anything, but in everything by prayer and supplication with thanksgiving let your requests be made known to God" (Philippians 4:6). Before God, we do not have to assume identities and postures that are forced or foreign to our essential makeup. Nor do we have to be concerned to observe this or that formality, avoid this or that pitfall, always doing the right thing for the right reason in the right way. Being who we are is the first requirement of prayer.

All the same, biblical faith enjoins us to avoid certain types of prayer just as it cautions us to eschew certain beliefs and activities. Not everything that people do in the name of prayer is simply condoned. Even when it is entirely sincere, prayer is sometimes inappropriate. When the Pharisee of the parable in Luke 18:10-14 thanked God that he was "not like other men," for instance "this tax-collector" here, he was being perfectly honest, altogether "himself." However, Jesus denounced such prayer because it was nothing more than a liturgical expression of human arrogance and self-righteousness, besides being altogether lacking in self-knowledge. Not only did the man fail to recognize that in God's presence "None is righteous, no, not one" (Romans 3:10); he was equally insensitive in relation to his fellow-worshipper, whose acknowledged unrighteousness was in fact more acceptable to God than the assumed righteousness of the Pharisee. Sincerity, though it is of course preferable to sham or halfheartedness, is thus no final criterion of authenticity where prayer is concerned. Other criteria are implicit in the Scriptures, and while the mercy and forebearance of God will, no doubt, cover a multitude of inappropriate prayers as it covers a multitude of sins, this does not provide faith with a license to indulge in whatever prayer comes into the head.

Throughout this study, we have been attempting to identify some of these other criteria. It will help us to summarize the substance of our findings here if we now turn our positive thoughts upside down and say what kinds of prayer would seem inappropriate, if the criteria for prayer implied in these discussions were to be observed.

Five types of inappropriate prayer are (1) Prayer that helps us escape from reality; (2) Prayer that turns us in upon ourselves and leaves us there; (3) Prayer that fails to represent our fellow-creatures, especially those in need; (4) Prayer that is merely emotional or lacking in serious, disciplined thought; (5) Prayer that does not lead to responsible acts of discipleship. These five do not exhaust the possibilities, but they can perhaps serve to remind us of the most salient points of the preceding discussion and at the same time lend a greater concreteness to that discussion.

Prayer That Helps Us Escape from Reality

There is, of course, a certain need to escape from a world that is burning (to use an image from the *Quo Vadis* legend alluded to earlier). It is somehow natural to want to get out of a dangerous situation. R. D. Laing and others who treat schizophrenia have pointed out that the schizophrenic reaction—the creation of a secondary world—is in a certain sense a sane reaction, or, more accurately, a form of insanity based upon a fundamentally sane impulse. For if the world is "sick," then the attempt to construct a more acceptable world in one's mind cannot be considered a wholly pathological response to reality. Perhaps it is more pathological when people simply accept the status quo, as though it were really acceptable.

In any case, we all know that the need to "get away from it all" belongs to our frenetic age. The busy lawyer or dentist flees to Switzerland to ski. The clergyperson, burdened day in and day out with the cares of others, is glad to vegetate before some mediocre film or lose himself or herself in an Agatha Christie mystery at the end of the day. Parents need to escape their children, thus creating the demand for whole "light industries": baby-sitting services, summer camps, and so forth. Children are equally in need of getting away from their home environment, as every wise parent knows. In Canada and the United States, the whole populace seems anxious to take to the road as soon as summer comes, and many people whose work is routine or meaningless to them live chiefly for this annual flight from the everyday.

The desire to escape is a fact of life, and it would be foolish for Christians to deny or ignore this fact. In the second chapter of this book, we attempted to recognize the importance of the escape factor and build it into our understanding of prayer. Prayer does mean getting away from it all. You have to stand off from your life in order to gain perspective on it. You have to find something like an Archimedean point outside the world in order to discern what is happening in the world, in order to move, alter, and change the world.

But the "in order to" in that sentence is of the utmost significance. Prayer that simply capitulates to the escape syndrome cannot stand the test of biblical faith. Not that the Bible knows nothing of the will to escape. In the Gethsemane prayer, Jesus himself gave expression to just that desire: ". . . if it is possible, let this cup pass from me" (paraphrase of Matthew 26:39). The reason for this is not hard to understand once we have grasped the Bible's most insistent claim, namely its commitment to life. The tradition of Jerusalem celebrates life and the goodness of creation, as we have seen. The desire to escape from this world is often born of the sense that the world as it is—as seen in the status quo—has missed the point.

Perhaps it is moving towards death, having "made a covenant with death" (Isaiah 28:15). Jesus in Gethsemane is affirming life when he prays that his apparent destiny might be altered. He does not go to his death as if death as such were a good or desirable thing. Nor does he encourage his followers to do so. Biblical faith is against death. Death is the enemy that must be conquered—it is the last enemy (1 Corinthians 15:26; Revelation 21:4). Stoicism, with which Christianity has sometimes been confused on this point, accepts death and devises techniques for spiritual resignation to death as to every other human fate. Biblical courage, unlike Stoic courage, always opts for life and wills to change what can be changed in order that life may be preserved and enhanced.

Prayer takes us a little way out of the world in order to put us back into it with new enthusiasm for its life and future and for our own lives in it. To pray for deliverance from life may be understandable and even good when nothing can be done to change the pain that has taken charge of a person's existence. Yet while individuals may be justified in asking God for the deliverance of death, this is not a Christian option when it comes to the world as a whole. When Christians and whole denominations and movements on this continent pray for the end of the world, they are giving expression to religious sentiments that cannot justify themselves as truly biblical, no matter how many isolated texts may be found to corroborate them, or how much twisting of the text that is there. (For alas, as Luther said, "The Bible has a wax nose." It is not difficult to twist its meaning.) The final words of the New Testament—"Come, Lord Jesus!" (Revelation 22:20)—do not translate into "Come, sweet Death." Jesus Christ is "the life of the world" (John 14:6),[52] not the harbinger of its demolition.

As I said earlier, I did not intend to write about the mechanics of prayer. I do not mean to alter that decision at this point, yet there are certain implicit directives for the practice of prayer in much that I have written here. The present observation states that the church draws apart from the world through its prayer as Jesus drew apart with his first disciples. However, the end effect of the church's prayer ought always to be what it also was for that first gathered community: to reorientate the disciple community to the world, to send it out again with a more vigorous and reflective hope, a better vision, a renewed sense of the worthwhileness of the human project. Too many of our traditional prayers and collects fail to do that. Our hymns are often notoriously otherworldly in their orientation:

Spirit of God, descend Upon my heart;
Wean it from earth. . . .

Given such sentiments, it is no wonder that those who have felt the greatest responsibility for earth and the most joy in their creatureliness have often found Christianity unsympathetic. Is that not because we have failed to reflect the creation-affirming, incarnational thrust of the gospel in our worship? This brings a serious challenge to all of us.

Prayer That Turns Us in Upon Ourselves

The Judeo-Christian tradition does not disclaim the significance of the self. No less than platonic philosophy, Christian faith counsels the human being to "Know thyself." Self-knowledge belongs to the encounter with God, the "I-Thou" encounter (Buber) where faith begins; and the acceptance of self is certainly one of the aims of the gospel. Contrary to forms of religion (including much historical Christianity) that court a sense of enduring guilt and preoccupation with the fate of the soul, biblical faith moves the human spirit towards an acceptance of the self through the knowledge of divine forgiveness and love.

Yet that is precisely why prayer that has the end result of turning us in upon ourselves has to be questioned. What God seems to desire of us, if we can take Jesus' summary of the Law at face value, is that we become sufficiently nonchalant about the self that we may begin really to see the others who surround us whose need is greater than our own, whose fate might even become so important to us that we would be ready to lay down our own lives for them (John 15:13). A self that is tied up in knots on account of its own evil or good, fixated on its personal destiny, absorbed by personal phobias or ambitions or likes and dislikes, is a self that is of little use to a God who commands us to love our neighbor. No doubt the Samaritan who encountered that poor wretch at the side of the road had problems and priorities of his own. But he was sufficiently liberated from preoccupation with his own existence that he was able to devote himself for several days to an absolute stranger. In this he was wholly unlike the other two travellers, both of them impeccably religious, whose self-absorption did not leave them the leeway needed for divine service.

The self is a great mystery, an entity full of both problems and possibilities. Without self-knowledge we can never achieve the fullness of creaturehood that God intends for us as human beings. The Pharisee of Jesus' parable (Luke 18:9-14) lacked self-knowledge. On the contrary, the man who came to Jesus asking about what good deed he might do in order to have eternal life (Luke 18:18-27) possessed an unusual degree of self-awareness. He knew that he was not good, that he could not boast in God's presence. He knew that he was missing something. However, it was his continued preoccupation with himself that made it impossible for him to follow and to be a disciple. He was too rich—too bound up with the treasures he had laid up on earth, in which he hoped to find security (Matthew 19:16-22).

There is no way into the great, wide world that does not pass through the little, narrow gateway of the self. In other words, we cannot really understand what the gospel is all about in its declaration of God's universal love unless we experience is personally. Without that personal sense of being grasped by a grace that will not let us go, grace, love, faith, and prayer, and all else remains at the level of theoretical knowledge.

But the self is a gateway, not the place into which the gateway permits us to go. Anyone who stood admiring a doorway that opens onto a banquet hall with a wonderful feast just ready to begin would rightly be regarded as a little odd. The kingdom of God is like a banquet (see Luke 14:15-24). One has to receive an invitation and one has to accept it. But once there, one becomes a part of something infinitely larger than oneself.

There is surely every reason why prayer, especially congregational prayer, should include the most personal matters. Prayer from which the self is absent, with all of its dreams and failures, is like a banquet to which only the most general sort of invitation is extended—nobody quite knows whether he or she actually belongs there. Through the little doorway of the self, with its microcosmic uncertainties, it is possible to enter the great world, the macrocosm, whose future is even more uncertain today than most of our own personal futures. Entering through that little doorway, we may learn how to become friends for the earth. But the minister or lay leader who leaves the congregation in the doorway may be as reprehensible, finally, as the one who forgot that every banquet hall has to have an entrance and every guest an invitation.

Prayer That Fails to Represent Others

It follows from the previous observation, and our discussion of prayer as an act of representation (chapter 4), that a failure to be present for others is a mark of inauthenticity in prayer. Prayers of intercession, as they have been called, are not incidental to the prayer of the congregation and of individual Christians. They are the essence of prayer when it is undertaken in the name of our mediator, Jesus Christ. It is not an act of special service, a sort of over-and-above, when the church intercedes for others. The truth is that the church would simply not have expressed its being as Christ's body in anything like fullness were it not to do this. Jesus did not pray for himself only, but also for others. This must be the direction of all Christian prayer, even when it is not explicitly called "intercessory." Christian prayer is intercessory by definition because it is the prayer of a priestly people.

Two observations need to be made in this connection. First, the intercessory nature of prayer ought not to be construed as if it were only an act of the intellect. Certainly it is not just a matter of naming names. Someone says to you, "Please remember me in your prayers," and so, next time you are in church or at your private devotions you say, dutifully enough, ". . . and please, God, remember X . . . ." You may go on to mention what X's problem is; if you are especially dutiful you may even go into some detail. Similarly, in church services we sometimes are subjected to long lists of first names (with or without details) whom we are to "remember before God." This may be necessary, especially in city congregations with their gaping impersonality and anonymity. But if individual Christians or congregations think that they have discharged their responsibilities as a priestly people when they have offered up such lists and reminders to God, they are surely missing some dimension of biblical faith.

That we can regard such remembering as intercession is, of course, symptomatic of a larger malaise by which contemporary, one-dimensional humanity is afflicted. This malaise can be called individualism, but it really is more complicated than that. It is a failure to perceive the world as a whole, a unity, in which every part is bound up with every other part. It is the shortsightedness of beings who have been so thoroughly insulated from nature by economic affluence and high technology that they are incapable of discerning their interconnectedness and interdependence in relation to all that is. We have the absolutely ungrounded impression that we are in a different situation from those for whom we intercede, as if they were passengers in another ship altogether. From the safety of our sanity, our cozy homes and churches, our youth and beauty, and our well-padded middle-age, we intercede for the handicapped, the infirm, the homeless, the aged, the poor, *et al*. Have we lost the imagination that it takes to see in the beggar at our gates our own human condition? Luther said, "We are [all] beggars." Do we suppose that we are immune to the hypertension that has afflicted our neighbor, the panic that has seized our business partner, the alcoholism that has cursed so many good homes, the drugs that have ruined young lives? Can we simply pray for these others, and not also pray with them, alongside them, *as* them? Dives' problem was just such a lack of imagination. In the long run, it proved no peccadillo. It landed him in hell (Luke 16:20-31)! Ecologists and many other students of the earth remind us today that our whole civilization may end in some hell if we are unable to recover a feeling for the interconnectedness of all things. They present for our grave consideration a secular parallel or a scientific version of the representational conception of human life and vocation contained explicitly in symbols like stewardship and priesthood. These ancient ideas are not just idiosyncracies of a religious tradition, they are dimensions of the Law of God, the "Maker of Heaven and Earth." We are one, and until we learn to live as one, we shall be in great peril.

Christian prayer is intercessory because it is the prayer of a priestly people, a people being brought into holy solidarity with all creatures, a people learning to pray that we "may all be one" (John 17:21). Those whom we remember in prayer are not in another ship—they are fellow passengers on a fragile craft. We are accountable for their journey, which is also our own journey. Representing them is not, after all, such an extraordinary feat of the human spirit. We already represent them, and they us; for we share a common being and a common pilgrimage. It is only a matter of overcoming our false impression of independence.

A second observation is that we have a tendency, particularly visible in this New World, towards privatism in religion. We sometimes manage to overcome our one-dimensionality long enough to intercede for individuals; but it is rare for Christians and especially for congregations to apply this same priestly logic to collectivities of other races and peoples. No doubt this reticence is due partly to an understandable and human difficulty of identifying with classes of things. We can often achieve a remarkable degree of empathy with particular persons, animals, or plants; yet we have difficulty transferring such compassion to the larger groupings of which these particular beings are members. This natural tendency to concentrate on particulars is complicated by our individualistic approach to life and our fear of mixing religion and politics.

Thus, while we have little difficulty praying for individual

South Africans, we are chary of incorporating into prayer, particularly at the congregational level, any suggestion that as Christians we ought to have solidarity with the black and colored races of that society. We also, of course, avoid the concommitant if only implicit suggestion that we should be critical of another race or class, the upholders of apartheid. Liberationists have insisted that the God of Abraham and of Jesus manifests a preferential option for the poor and oppressed. The reason why Isaiah's God will not listen even if the people make many prayers is that their hands are covered with blood. They have not sought justice or corrected oppression. They have been "grinding the face of the poor" (Isaiah 3:15). For similar reasons, Jeremiah is commanded not to pray for this people (Jeremiah 7:16, 11:4), and the psalmist complains that God is "angry with thy people's prayers" (Psalm 80:4).

The representation of others in prayer means others in all the reality of their private and public life. Somehow, even if it requires that our congregational prayers begin to sound seditious to some who make the separation of religion and politics a divine mandate, we shall have to learn how to represent whole groupings of humans in our prayers. Otherwise, our prayers for individuals, including ourselves, will be less than meaningful or real. No individual lives in isolation from social and political structures, and even to begin to grasp the oppression of millions of private persons in our world will carry us by that same helping Spirit into the political arena again and again.

Prayer That Is Deficient in Serious and Disciplined Thought

There is an unwritten law that is strongly operative among Protestants of the Free Church variety in particular that has it that the primary ingredient in prayer is feeling. This leads to the notion that spontaneity in prayer is considered so essential that clergy and others who actually prepare their prayers in advance are often considered unspiritual or lacking in devotional ardor. Prayer should pour forth uninhibited by the mind, apparently, as soon as the magic words, "Let us pray," are uttered. Even hesitation of speech becomes suspect in such circles. Perhaps the person praying is thinking too much between phrases!

Let me preface what I will say about the inappropriateness of such prayer with a sincere acknowledgment of the importance of emotions in the life of faith. An emotionless faith is a contradiction in terms. Anyone who can repeat the Psalms without emotion is either spiritually dead or lacking in plain intelligence. The language of the Scriptures is filled with words of passion often attributed to the divine Being. This is evident in the Isaiah passage quoted at the beginning of this chapter:

> New moon and sabbath and the
> calling of assemblies—
> I cannot endure iniquity and
> solemn assembly.
> Your new moons and your appointed
> feasts
> my soul hates. . . .—Isaiah 1:13-14

"Hate" is very strong language! So is love. And God is love! Who can think about the love, hate, justice, wrath, mercy, judgment, and forgiveness of God without feeling? What scholar is so devoid of vested interests that he or she can engage in a detailed exegesis of the passion of the Christ with nary a sigh or groan? The answer, alas, is far too many. But what is the price of scholarship of that kind? Is it, perhaps, the truth? Truth moves one! Truth "wounds from behind" (Kierkegaard) even when it does not move the heart openly. To be detached before the truth is an absurd idea.

However, the banishment of the quest for truth and understanding for fear that such a quest might detract from the spontaneity of faith is just as absurd. In fact, when spontaneity and feeling are pursued independent of the quest for truth they become bogus. Emotion is one thing. Emotion is never present apart from some sort of brush with truth. Emotionalism is another matter. Like all "isms," it is pursued for its own sake. People like to have the effects of truth without the pain of searching for it or finding it. So they imitate the emotions of those who are truly worshipping God in spirit and in truth.

How much emotionalism is associated with the practice of prayer in our church and society? Emotions are conjured up and mocked. It is a disgusting thing when this happens, whether it is in bad drama or in television evangelism. The special facial features, the forced tears and sobs and catches in the voice, the gestures, the stereotypical handclasping and unctuous speech—all of it is a pathetic shortcut to the emotions that really belong to faith.

There is no shortcut. Only the frivolous can be moved by the pseudoemotional. True emotion is inseparable from the search for and experience of truth. This means that the mind, far from being dormant in the act of prayer, is called upon precisely in that act to perform at its most exacting—before, during, and after the act.

The form of public prayer is not my concern here. There are positive things to be said for extemporaneous prayer and also for prepared prayers such as the historic collects and litanies of the more liturgical traditions. I see no reason why there should not be great variety in the practice of congregational prayer. Regardless of the form, however, what informs prayer, whether directly or indirectly, must be prolonged and disciplined thought. It must be a serious attempt on the part of ministers and people to find reason for their hope. Without this, the so-called prayer life, both of individuals and worshipping communities, devolves into rote pomposity or sheer emotional froth, predictability of style and content, and mere wordiness. "And in praying," said, Jesus, "do not heap up empty phrases as the Gentiles do; for they think that they will be heard for their many words" (Matthew 6:7). Jesus then presents his model, the Lord's Prayer, which, if carefully scrutinized[53] implies every major theme of biblical faith. This indicates that it is the prayer of a real rabbi, who knew very intimately the traditions of his faith and was ready to give a reason for it.

Prayer That Does Not Lead to Responsible Discipleship

After all that has been noted about the inseparability of thought, word, and deed, it would be superfluous to engage in an extended discussion of the inappropriateness of prayer that ends with the "Amen." At the same time, we cannot leave this out of account. It is necessary to say that genuine prayer leads through thought and word to deed and back again, in an unceasing circle of reflection and action. It is also necessary to say that prayer that does not do this is ungenuine and inappropriate.

What I mean is that the failure to move towards the enactment of prayer is not always intentional. One would suppose, given the Bible's constant warnings against unfulfilled promises of obedience, that the failure to pray as though the deed were simply a necessary dimension of the thought is usually not intentional. In fact, it is more likely habitual. It is a deficiency of imagination as much as, if not more than, a willful avoidance of obedience.

In Jesus' parable of Matthew 21:28-32, did the son who told his father that he would certainly go to the vineyard and work, and then didn't, remain at home in the shade out of pure willfulness? Possibly. None of us is above making promises that we do not intend to keep. How many congregations really mean it when they promise, at baptisms or receptions for new members to uphold the subjects of these offices? Yet it also is possible that the son in question simply was in the habit of saying yes to whatever his father asked of him. He was like the elder son in the parable of the prodigal son who simply stayed at home and did the expected thing, no more and no less. It would occur to neither of these parabolic sons to rebel or to create a scene by saying, "No, I won't go!" "No, I probably won't raise a finger to see the future Christian education of these children being baptized!"

There are sins of omission where all of this is concerned. It is not only a matter of downright disobedience when we fail to "act justly" and thus complete our prayer with an amen that means something. People say what is expected of them. If generations of Christians convey the impression that not much is expected of them, except that they say the right words and go through the right motions, then it is a little unfair when people like me chastise "ordinary" Christians for failing to follow through with the promises they make in prayer to live more nearly as they pray.

Has not the time come when all of us who bear responsibility for the edification of the faithful shall have to become more direct and more informative about the practical implications of prayer? Centuries of Christian establishment, legal or cultural, have conditioned Christian people to sit lightly to everything that the New Testament calls discipleship. Since everyone was Christian simply by being born; and Christian principles would be observed since the nation itself was Christian; since the young would quite naturally seek confirmation (after sowing their "wild oats"); and since everyone would as a matter of course present themselves to the church for marriage, Communion, and burial—what could there be to complain about?

But the enthusiastic claims of evangelists and periodic upswings in religion notwithstanding, Christendom is over. That form of the church, which biblical ecclesiology could call in question long before Kierkegaard did, has had its day. Whether we like it or not, and regardless of the fact that cultural Christianity is still able to make a very big noise on this continent, we are today a *diaspora* church in a religiously and culturally pluralistic society. There are no more automatic Christians, and what happens in the name of Christianity cannot be trusted at face value.

What this means, to be intensely practical, is that we all shall have to begin "to live more nearly as we pray," because the follow-through of prayer is not going to happen automatically.

It never did, really, but the illusion was pervasive. Certainly God has other hands and feet, other disciples who are "not of this fold" (John 10:16)—including some who insist that they do not believe in God and announce that they will not go! But the providence of God can no longer function as an excuse for our lack of radical obedience. We all shall have to learn that prayer is only a dimension of a life that is all-embracing in its vocation to divine service in a world sorely in need of workers in the vineyard.

Conclusion

Turn to Me,
and Live

"Why will you die, O house of Israel? For I have no pleasure in the death of any one, says the Lord GOD; so turn, and live"
(Ezekiel 18:31-32).

. . . until we all attain to . . . mature [humanity], to the measure of the stature of the fulness of Christ . . . (Ephesians 4:13-16).

In the oral traditions and lore of many ancient tribes of the earth, there appears a legend in which every child who is about to be born is asked whether it wishes to enter the world. Is it not perhaps too comfortable in the warm, dark, and holy place that is the womb of its mother? Does it really wish to leave that secure nest and enter this cold and uncertain sphere? Does it wish to subject its gentle, untried senses to the penetrating light and the alarming noises of the earth, to learn the hard lessons of survival, to toil toward acceptance and human warmth, to face tragedies and temptations, possibly to fail, certainly to die? Very often, the legend relates, the child hesitates for a long time before consenting to be born. Sometimes it determines to remain in that warm place, refusing to come out. Then it must be forced to leave—but sometimes it will not leave, living, even then.

This ancient folk wisdom, which Freud and his followers improved upon only by classifying it in the mythic language of science, contains an abiding truth about the human condition: the greatest temptation of human life is to refuse life.

There are a great many ways in which this temptation is yielded to. Few of them are obvious. Most of us are able to resist the more direct proposals of the Tempter, the "Thief of Life," as he was named in the seventeenth-century Roman Catholic order of exorcism set forth by Pope Paul V.[54] To be attracted by deliberate death is, to be sure, not unusual. Freud's famous *Todestrieb* (the death wish) is not confined to the few who take their own lives. Käthe Kollwitz, one of the great artists of our era, was branded "enemy of the people" by the Nazis because of her refusal to depict only what was beautiful in the German nation. She made a charcoal drawing of herself in rapt conversation with Death entitled "Gespräch mit dem Tod." On the face of this woman, who was exceptionally committed to life, was a look of one almost persuaded.

Persons who know themselves are not surprised by this look. The Thief of Life is a visitor to all our lives, and sometimes he is half-welcomed.

> To die: to sleep;
> To sleep: perchance to dream: ay, there's the rub;
> For in that sleep of death what dreams may come
> When we have shuffled off this mortal coil,
> Must give us pause. . . .[55]

Yet the majority of us resist the pull of oblivion by expending a good deal of effort to keep it from surfacing in our conscious thought. It does not follow from this, however, that we resist the basic temptation to refuse life. The Tempter has far more subtle proposals up his sleeve than suicide.

To redesign life according to one's own patterns, to cause one's environment to serve one's own obdurate will, to invent an alternative world—is this not also to refuse life as it is offered by the Spirit, "the Lord and Giver of life?" We do not love the world God made, with its small circumscriptions of our vaunted freedom, so we try to make it over. Our cities defy the laws of nature. Our technology turns winter into summer. Our medicine ensures longevity. Perhaps death itself will be conquered by our ingenuity. Our knowledge enables us to have the kind of dominion over all other creatures that the ancient priestly author of Genesis could not have dreamt of. We have become gods—creators in our own right.

And if our cities become ungovernable, our technology gives us stones instead of bread, our medicine serves to prolong life in bodies that have lost any reason to be, our dominion of others threatens to overwhelm our own species, subjecting our lives to the same constraints that we have placed upon other forms of life, then perhaps we are ready to entertain a more subtle though tried and true temptation from the Thief of Life: religion! Since this world refuses to transform itself to our conceptions of what is acceptable, we shall transfer our affections to another realm. We desire—we deserve—gates of pearl and streets of gold. We cannot settle for this inferior little planet with its rampant and disordered vegetation, its species all preying upon one another, its unspeakable natural limitations, and perverse citizenry. Undoubtedly we shall have to live here in the meantime, but let us live as strangers and sojourners, as citizens of another, better country, until real life begins.

This is, of course, the Tempter's master stroke, offered in variations on the theme to every reflective soul. The temptation was offered to Adam and Eve, in whose spirits the Thief of Life first planted dissatisfaction with the world, though it was a veritable garden. It was offered to the "second Adam," too, for all the temptations of the wilderness were proposals to defy and disregard the laws of the world that has been offered us. The final temptation of Gethsemane and the Cross—to resort to unearthly power, to call forth legions of angels, to come down from the cross—is the same. The Tempter, though "father of lies" (John 8:44), knows well the place where God's creatures are most vulnerable. Why would he not know it? He, too, is God's creature and servant. The Tempter is a fallen creature and a reluctant servant, to be sure; yet he knows much about the construction of the thinking animal. There is a fine line of distinction between the dissatisfaction that is born of the God-given vision that "earth might be fair and all her folk be one," and the dissatisfaction that is a by-product of the refusal to accept the gift of life. Faith is fed by the first dissatisfaction, for it is God's own invitation to covenant partnership in the building of the kingdom. The second is the tacit decision that the kingdom cannot be built here on earth as it is built in heaven. It is this dissatisfaction that nourishes the religious quest, from Babel to our glass cathedrals and communications towers; and it is just this that inspired the young Barth to cry that the message of the Bible is that God hates religion.[56]

How hard it is for those rich in great expectations and rich in comforts to enter life. The voice of the Tempter repeatedly asks us, "But do you really want to be born?" True, we have by one means or another overcome our initial inhibitions. We were taken from the womb alive. We did as little children leave our homes daily to make our uncertain way among our peers. We have (perhaps) opened ourselves to a few other human beings, taken certain risks, and ventured into unfamiliar scenes. Still, life keeps offering itself to us in ever new and more demanding forms. Life will have us leave the nest again and again, like Abraham, going out into the unknown. It will lift us clear out of the familiar patterns and routines, the circles and classes of persons in whose midst we at least have found security if not actual acceptance. It will introduce us to unwelcome strangers: to poor Lazaruses at our gates, to victims of the technological society languishing by the roadside of life, to street people, to women demanding equal rights, to refugees, and to sufferers with AIDS and other diseases. Life will forever invade our minds, expanding our imaginations, driving us towards greater and still less manageable truth. If we followed life we might, like old Faust, grow discouraged and say, "I now do see that we can nothing know." Life wants to carry us further into the mystery of the interior, and we are terrified. Who knows where such a journey would lead? Who can say what humiliations and deprivations it would entail? One might even lose one's life on such a wild adventure. Better to remain here in this womb.

"Follow me!"

Is it Life who calls? Yes, it is the very Source of Life, its Alpha and Omega. However, this one who is the Life is also the Way. His invitation is no mere command. Many who have surrounded us from our youth command and exhort and cajole: we should come to life, begin to live, get with it. It is easy to issue commands. To provide a way is something else.

His way is the way of the cross. The wisdom of the world considers it very strange indeed that the way to life would have to pass through death. "How very strange!" cry the worldly-wise, that the One who claims to offer life in abundance leads his unlikely flock along the Via Dolorosa, into forsakenness, suffering and rejection, and the companionship of thieves and harlots. Can such a thing be life?

"For whoever would save his life will lose it; and whoever loses his life for my sake and the gospel's will save it" (Mark 8:35). So responds the One who is the world's Light and Life, uttering paradox upon paradox, mystery upon mystery. All the same, the unborn soul knows full well what is meant. There, in the cozy darkness of its womb, it is trying to save its life. That is the only reason why the unborn soul hesitates and refuses to come out. The womb, the home, the office, and the sanctuary all feel so safe. Why should the unborn soul relinquish all that—especially when what is offered is a hard and bitter way? Yet it can not live forever in that womb. It will suffocate. It will be starved. It will die before it has begun to live. It is ripe to be born, wanting to be born, waiting, poised for life, impelled from contractions within and beckonings without. The only alternative to the costly life that is offered it is stillbirth. It will never know the chance to test its lungs, limbs, and brain. It will remain at the stage of potentiality, stunted in its spiritual growth, malformed of soul, "a sword for cutting daisies" (Tennessee Williams). So many unborn souls people the earth! We need not speak so much of being born again. Few enough of us have completed the first birth. Our souls are still lingering in the womb.

"Come to me, all who labor and are heavy laden, and I will give you rest. Take my yoke upon you, and learn from me; for I am gentle and lowly in heart, and you will find rest for your souls. For my yoke is easy, and my burden is light" (Matthew 11:28-30).

How we distort this invitation when we turn it into an inducement to reject the life of creation in favor of "something better"! We act as if it were a challenge to remain in the womb when what it really is is an invitation to come out into the world and be born. It is not different in essence from that other form of the invitation: "If any man would come after me, let him deny himself and take up his cross and follow me" (Matthew 16:24). The invitation to discipleship is nothing more nor less than an invitation to life. It is not issued to that within each of us that is looking for a way of insulating ourselves even more securely from the life of the world, but to that which is waiting for a reason and a way to enter life. Heavy laden, not because life is too hard for us, but because our fear of living is so great. We cower before the sheer beauty and terror of conscious existence, lacking the nerve actually to say yes to life.

What is the gospel of the One whose burden is easy if not the gift of courage to be born, to come out into life? What is faith if not the acceptance of that gift? "He who through faith is [made right] shall live" (Galatians 3:11). What is prayer if not the means by which we daily appropriate the gift? "Give us this day our daily bread" (Matthew 6:11).

This bread of life has to be received daily, like the manna of the wilderness. It cannot be stored up. Besides, our hunger is never assuaged and our anxiety about tomorrow is never fully calmed. The Thief of Life, too, is active to the very end. "Shall we never be fully alive?" to quote Irenaeus.[57] Shall we always lack the "measure of the stature of the fulness of Christ," (4:13) of which the writer of Ephesians speaks so wonderfully? Shall we never complete the journey into the interior? Shall we never finish thinking our way into God's beloved world?

Perhaps not. Perhaps it has to be enough for us that the way goes on, and that we are permitted to follow it with thanksgiving. Perhaps the telos, the fullness of living, will only come later.

But let us not be led along that route to some exalted worldlessness that keeps us from thinking our way into God's world! There are intimations of maturity all along the way. It is only a matter of being alert and knowing what to watch for.

Two such intimations of maturity follow. They may be parables in their way. One of them concerns a very young person, the other a man of many years—for the maturity in question has little to do with age.

*   *   *

"What do you want to be?" asked an elderly gentleman of his seventeen-year-old nephew. They had been considering the future of the young man. The uncle, a man of the world, practical, though in his way a romantic, thought it high time to put the question to his young charge. "Well then, what do you want to be when you grow up?"

The boy hesitated, his brow furrowed. He was an active, spirited adolescent with a slightly apocryphal reputation for mischief-making: He had begun to love music, especially Mozart. He wanted to play the "Clarinet Concerto" well.

"Well, what are you thinking about? What do you want to be?"

"I want," said the boy at last, "I want to be human."

The uncle was astonished—perhaps secretly also a little

proud. "That's all very well," he spluttered. "We all want to have a good time—we all want to be 'human,' as you put it. But what are you going to do? How will you make a living?"

"I don't know," the boy admitted, honestly enough. "But whatever I shall *do,* I want to *be* human."

*   *   *

"According to the Bible," said the old man with a knowing twinkle, "people used to live to be hundreds of years old. Then somebody had the idea that it was too much, so they decided to limit human life to a hundred-and-twenty."

He paused. I looked at him sitting there, smiling up at me. I was a mere youngster in his view. Seeing him made me think—as I usually thought in his presence—of that beautiful Jewish toast, "L'chaim!" (To Life!) He had been a lawyer in Moscow. His father had been a reader in the great synagogue, the only one that remains in all of Moscow today. Since coming to North America eight years earlier, he had learned French and English, written books and articles, furnished a house with treasures from garage sales, consulted with prisoners and directors of broadcasting systems, invented a number of labor-saving devices, become intimate with a large circle of friends, and taken out citizenship in his new nation.

I am now," he continued, "seventy-five years old. With a hundred-and twenty, it means I still have forty-five years left." He laughed aloud.

"It's not too much!"

Notes

Introduction

*The RSV, more accurately, reads "kingship."

[1]Karl Barth, *Prayer and Preaching*, trans. Sara F. Terrien and B. E. Nooke (London: S.C.M. Press, 1964), p. 20.

[2]The reader's attention is drawn to two, perhaps hidden aspects of this sentence. First, the attribution of maleness to the deity—God "himself." While I shall intentionally avoid exclusive language in my own text, it is important to recognize that sexist terminology applied to God in certain Christian circles is not merely a matter of habit. It is an inescapable doctrinal consequence of precisely this one-sided accentuation of the divinity of Jesus as the Christ. If Jesus is God—he is God—then one can hardly avoid the conclusion that God is indeed a "he!"

Second, the sentence contains (intentionally) an implicit denigration of the Old Testament and the living religion of Israel. To use the technical term, it is implicitly "supersessionist," meaning that the New Covenant is understood to supercede the old. This, too, shows the inherent propensity of Christian theology to place an inordinate emphasis upon Jesus' divinity. If you say that Jesus was God, then, even though you may give all kinds of lip service to the authority of the Hebraic Scriptures for Christians, you automatically relegate to the status of the preliminary and inferior all of those who from Moses to Malachi bore witness to the truth of God. Being human, and even all-too-human, they cannot match the One whose essence is his deity.

The time has long since passed when Christians can write and think about Jesus and pray through him without considering the implications of what they say for those whom "Christianity" has oppressed.

[3]John L. Casteel, *Rediscovering Prayer* (New York: Association Press, 1955). See especially the final chapter, "Growth in Prayer."

[4]"On the Incarnation," in *Christology of the Later Fathers, Library of Christian Classics*, Edward Rochie Hardy, ed. (London: S.C.M. Press) vol. 3, pp. 55 ff.

[5]See Barth's essay, "The Humanity of God," in *The Humanity of God,* trans. John Newton Thomas and Thomas Wieser (Richmond: John Knox Press, 1960), pp. 37 ff.

[6]Abraham Heschel, *The Prophets of Israel* (New York: Harper and Row, Publishers Inc., 1962), p. 225.

[7]Dietrich Bonhoeffer, *The Cost of Discipleship* (New York: Macmillan Publishing Co., 1963).

[8]This characterization of the *agape* of God comes from the classical study of Anders Nygren, Bishop of Lund; Philip S. Watson, trans., *Agape and Eros* (Philadelphia: The Westminster Press, 1953).

[9]Harold S. Kushner, *When Bad Things Happen to Good People* (New York: Avon Books, 1983).

[10]Paul Tillich, *The Shaking of the Foundations* (New York: Charles Scribner's Sons, 1948), pp. 153 ff.

[11]This legend is found in the apocryphal Acts of Peter. The story says that Peter, now in Rome and facing the terrifying persecutions to which the first Christians were subjected, determined to make his way out of that city as quickly as possible. This was an understandable reaction, as Peter was always a survivor. But along the Appian Way he had a powerful vision of the crucified Christ, going into the city. "Domine, quo vadis?" ("Where are you going, Lord?") asked the astonished foundation-stone of the church. "Into the city," replied Jesus, "to be crucified again." Whereupon Peter, recognizing once more his propensity to deny the Christ and save his own skin, repented, turned, and went back into Rome, himself to be crucified.

The legend is, of course, a legend. But theologically it is altogether true. World-denial and the denial of Christ are, for the tradition of Jerusalem, virtually the same thing. It is to make us human that God suffered the destiny of humanity, not to lift us out of burning creation but to place us more concretely within it. The legend also is true in its accurate reflection of the church in this disciple, this "foundation-stone" whose constant temptation was to turn the Word of the cross into one of worldly glory and thus to avoid the real plight of the human city.

[12]See the early essay of Karl Barth entitled, "The Strange, New World Within the Bible." Karl Barth, *The Word of God and the Word of Man,* trans. Douglas Horton (New York: Harper and Row, Publishers Inc., 1957), pp. 28 ff.

[13]Emil L. Fackenheim, *To Mend the World: Foundations of Future Jewish Thought* (New York: Schocken Books, Inc. 1982).

[14]The best of modern psychiatry has grasped this. In 1932, addressing the Alsatian Pastoral Conference at Strasbourg, Carl Jung said: ". . . we must first tread with the patient the path of his illness—the path of his mistake that sharpens his conflict and increases his loneliness till it becomes unbearable—hoping that from the psychic depths which cast up the powers of destruction the rescuing forces will also come." R. F. C. Hull, trans., and Sir Herbert Read, *et. al.*, eds., *The Collected Works of Carl G. Jung,*, vol. 11, Bollingen Series XX (Princeton, N. J.: Princeton University Press, 1958), Chapter 1, pp. 344-345.

Chapter 1

[15]As one of the foremost of these Christian socialists reminds us, however, the adjective "great" is inappropriate where theologians are concerned. There might have been great anatomists . . . or musicians . . . but great theologians is strictly a contradiction in terms. As theologians we can never be great, but at best we can only be small in our own way. The whole idea is impossible." Karl Barth, *A Karl Barth Reader,* ed. Rolf Joachim Erler and Reiner Marquart (Grand Rapids: Wm. B. Eerdmans Publishing Co., 1986), p. 113.

[16]Machovec writes: "No one doubts that Catholics and Protestants, the Orthodox and the

sects have a right to confess his name; but not only does it transpire on closer examination that the 'rebels' of this bimillenary history—'heretics' and 'atheists,' especially Marxists and Communists in more recent times—are in their own way an organic part of European history in which the Prophet from Nazareth once, and therefore indelibly, played such a significant part: one may even wonder whether the disciples of Karl Marx, who 1800 years after Jesus set in motion a similarly far-reaching and complex process with as yet quite unforeseeable consequences but similar aspirations to a radical transformation of social relationships and a future conceived in a radically different way, have not in fact the greatest right to regard themselves as the authentic perpetuators of Old Testament Messianism and early Christian desires for radical change. Many Marxists, but also many self-critical modern theologians, are aware of the fact that concern for the future—that longing for liberation and radical change once found in Christianity—has been taken over in the modern period almost exclusively by Marxism." Milan Machovec (*A Marxist Looks At Jesus* (Philadelphia: Fortress Press, 1976), p. 193.

[17] The whole statement in which this famous sentence is contained deserves to be better known than it is. "Religious distress," Marx wrote, "is at the same time the expression of real distress and the protest against real distress. Religion is the sigh of the oppressed creature, the heart of a heartless world, just as it is the spirit of an unspiritual situation. It is the opium of the people." Excerpt from "Toward the Critique of Hegel's Philosophy of Right" in Lewis S. Feuer, ed., *Karl Marx and Friedrich Engels: Basic Writings on Politics and Philosophy* (New York: Doubleday Publishing Co., 1959), p. 263. Marx's basic sympathy for the religious response to existence can be readily detected in this statement. As the subsequent sentence indicates, however, he did not perceive the religious response as a genuine resolution of the "distress" of the human condition, but (like Freud) a repressive mechanism for acquiring a bogus form of happiness. Therefore, "The abolition of religion as the illusory happiness of the people is required for their real happiness." An excellent commentary on Marx's text, given from the perspective of Christian belief, is found in Nicholas Lash, *A Matter of Hope: A Theologian's Reflections on the Thought of Karl Marx* (Notre Dame, Indiana: University of Notre Dame Press, 1982), pp. 158 ff.

[18] Douglas J. Hall, *Lighten Our Darkness: Toward an Indigenous Theology of the Cross* (Philadelphia: The Westminster Press, 1976).

[19] This statement, which appears on Marx's tombstone in London, is his eleventh thesis on the thought of Ludwig Feuerbach. It reads: "The philosophers have only interpreted the world, in various ways; the point, however, is to change it" (Feuer, ed., *Marx and Engels,* p. 245). See also Dorothee Söelle, *Political Theology,* trans. John Shelley (Philadelphia: Fortress Press, 1974), pp. 73 ff.: "For him [Marx] there is no such thing as a truth that can be acquired in detached, contemplative observation; the relation to truth . . . is determined by its interest in life. Marx says in the second thesis [on Feuerbach]: 'In praxis man must prove the truth, that is, the actuality and power and this-sidedness, of this thinking.' Political theology enters precisely here, because it grasps the relation to truth no longer as one of contemplation and theory only, as accords with the Greek mind, but as an operative and practical relation found not only in John but even more in the proclamation of Jesus."

[20] It is remarkable that this little prayer, "dashed off" by Niebuhr for use in a service of worship, has achieved such popular acclaim—to the point that its authorship is not known by thousands of people who use it. That this is so speaks for the universal appeal of the sentiments which the prayer so directly and unpretentiously voices. Not only alcoholics (the prayer is widely used by Alcoholics Anonymous) but also all of us know that there are some things that cannot be changed, and some that can and must be changed. The biases of academics notwithstanding, very "ordinary people" also recognize that the most difficult thing of all is to "discern the difference between them."

Chapter 2

[21]The Niebuhr prayer.

[22]It is not accidental, for example, that the eighteenth century, the Age of Reason *par excellence*, was also the age of deism. Deism was perhaps the most rationalistic explanation of God and the world, in quasi-Christian terms, ever to be advanced. Over against this, Wesley and Zinzendorf and others set their religion of the heart.

[23]Douglas J. Hall, "The Cross and Contemporary Culture," in *Reinhold Niebuhr and the Issues of Our time*, ed., Richard Harries (Grand Rapids, Wm. B. Eerdmans Publishing Co., 1986); and London and Oxford, Mowbray, 1986); pp. 183 ff.

Chapter 3

[24]Paul Tillich, *A History of Christian Thought: (Cambridge, Mass.: Peter H. John, 1956), p. 35.*

[25]Douglas J. Hall, *God and Human Suffering: An Exercise in the Theology of the Cross* (Minneapolis: Augsburg Publishing House, 1986). See chapter 2: "Creation—Suffering as Becoming."

[26]Fackenheim, *To Mend the World*.

[27]Vernon Sproxton, *Teilhard de Chardin* (Naperville, Ill.: Allenson Inc., 1971), p. 46.

[28]Teilhard de Chardin, *The Prayer of the Universe*, trans. Rêne Hague (New York: Harper and Row, Publishers Inc., 1973), p. 45.

[29]Elisabeth Young-Bruehl, *Hannah Arendt: For Love of the World*), New Haven, Conn.: Yale University Press, 1982), p. 498. (The statements in both double and single quotation marks are Arendt's own, cited from her work, *The Human Condition*.

[30]Kenneth Leech, *True Prayer: An Introduction to Christian Spirituality* (Toronto: Anglican Book Centre, 1980), p. 268.

[31]*Ibid.*

[32]For a discussion of this subject, see Williston Walker, *A History of the Christian Church*, ed. Robert T. Handy (New York: Charles Scribner's Sons, 1970), pp. 55-56.

[33]At the Council of Toledo in A.D. 589, the word *filioque* was added to the creed, causing it to read, "And I believe in the Holy Spirit . . . who proceedeth from the Father and the Son." This so-called dogma of the "Double Procession" of the Spirit became a point of contention between the Eastern and Western branches of Christendom.

[34]Dylan Thomas, *Collected Poems of Dylan Thomas* (New York: New Directions Publishing Corp., 1955), p. 21.

[35]"The Incarnation is a making new, a restoration, of all the universe's forces and powers: Christ is the instrument, the center, the end, of the whole of animate and material creation; through him, everything is created, sanctified, and vivified." (Teilhard de Chardin, *The Prayer of the Universe*. p. 91.)

[36]Benjamin G. Smillie, *Blessed Unrest: Prayers for Daily Living* (Winnipeg: Ronald P. Frye and Co., Publishers, 1985), p. 75.

Chapter 4

[37]See also 1 Corinthians 15:28; Ephesians 1:23; Colossians 3:11. The question is not whether Christianity is universalistic or not. God is under no obligation to fulfill a theory in which "all" are redeemed, as Karl Barth put it. Yet is is beyond doubt, surely, that the *intention* of God (who "is love") is to save all; and therefore the idea of an elite is excluded.

[38]Douglas J. Hall, *The Steward: A Biblical Symbol Come of Age* (New York: Friendship Press, 1982.)

[39]Teilhard de Chardin, *The Prayer of the Universe,* p. 99.

[40]Ibid., pp. 99-100

Chapter 5

[41]Dietrich Bonhoeffer, *Letters and Papers from Prison*, ed. E. Bethge (New York: Macmillan Publishing Co., 1967), p. 300.

[42]An interesting corroboration of this characterization is found in the speech patterns and diction associated with the type of prayer under discussion. Surely something is amiss when Canadian evangelicals, with their hard, clipped, northern accents, suddenly give way to the long, seductive vowels and drawl of southern and southwestern Americans as soon as they address their Lord and Savior!

[43]C. P. Snow, *The Two Cultures: And a Second Look* (Toronto: New American Library of Canada Limited, a Mentor Book, 1964).

[44]Nominalism refers to that theory of knowledge that denies reality to universal concepts and asserts that universals (tree, justice, humankind) are only names [*nomen*] that we give to classifications of things. The practical implications of this theory of knowledge for theology were great. Since the human mind can be said to "know" only particular things (trees, just deeds, specific human beings), it is not capable of discerning the reality that lies behind the particulars—including God. Thus belief in God is possible only on the basis of faith.

Chapter 6

[45]The German word for "Enlightenment" is in some ways more descriptive of what the leaders of this movement thought they were doing: *Aufklärung*—"clearing up." They were clearing up the debris of centuries of religion and superstition, they thought, and arranging everything according to the light of reason.

[46]Jacques Ellul, *The Technological Society* (New York: Alfred A. Knopf, Inc., 1964), p. 16.

[47]Paul Tillich, *Systematic Theology* (Chicago: University of Chicago Press, 1951), vol. 1, pp. 71-77.

[48]Martin Heidegger, *Discourse on Thinking* trans. John M. Anderson and E. Hans Freund (New York: Harper and Row, Publishers Inc., 1966).

[49]Douglas J. Hall, "Beyond Cynicism and Credulity: On the Meaning of Christian Hope," in *The Princeton Seminary Bulletin*, vol. 6, no. 3, (N. S. 1985), pp. 201 ff.

Chapter 7

[50]Feuer, ed., *Marx and Engels*.

[51] "All prayer is Kingdom-centered because it is oriented towards the coming of the 'age to come,' on earth as in heaven. All prayer is social, because it is rooted in *koinonia,* sharing, in the life of God. And all prayer is therefore political, because it is an essential element in the transformation of the world." (Kenneth Leech, *True Prayer,* p. 89).

Chapter 8

[52]The theme of the meeting of the World Council of Churches in Vancouver, B.C., in 1984.

Conclusion

[54]See the 1947 New York edition of the *Rituale Romanum*, with an introduction by Francis, Cardinal Spellman. This reproduced verbatim the rite as printed by Marimilian van Eynatten in 1619, and included in the *Thesaurus Exorcismorum.*

[55]William Shakespeare, *Hamlet,* Act 3, Scene 1.

[56]Karl Barth, *The Epistle to the Romans,* trans. Edwyn C. Hoskyns (New York and Don Mills, Ont.: Oxford University Press, 1950). See especially chapter 7. With his characteris-

tic incisiveness and a prophetic acumen that is as pertinent in North America today as it was in Europe fifty years ago, Barth wrote: ". . . just as genuine coins are open to suspicion so long as false coins are in circulation, so the perception which proceeds outwards from God cannot have free course until the arrogance of religion be done away" (p. 37).
[57]*Gloria Dei vivens homo.*